COOKING WITH MASTER CHEFS

COOKING WITH MASTER CHEFS

To Elaine

Julia Child

JULIA CHILD

Alfred A. Knopf New York 1993

This Is a Borzoi Book
Published by Alfred A. Knopf, Inc.

Copyright © 1993 by A La Carte Communications
Photographs copyright © 1993 by Fred Maroon, Micheal McLaughlin, Penina Meisels,
Barry Michlin, and Steven Minkowski

Library of Congress Cataloging-in-Publication Data
Child, Julia.
     Cooking with master chefs / written by Julia Child.—
1st ed.

          p.   cm.
     Includes index.
     ISBN 0-679-42993-X
     ISBN 0-679-74829-6 (pbk.)
     1. Cookery.   I. Title.
TX652.C495   1993
641.5—dc20   93-20241
                                                         CIP

Manufactured in the United States of America

First Edition

Contents

Introduction

When Geoffrey Drummond, the producer of our "Master Chefs" television series, first discussed his new TV project of working with professional chefs across America, I said I loved the idea because it had always been my hope that one day I could do just that. On my first TV series, "The French Chef," I had wanted to have guest chefs, but we never did. Now I was delighted to be involved with the planning and filming of a cooking series where chefs were put into home kitchens, using home equipment, and family-size rather than restaurant quantities. Professionals have so much to teach us when they have time to slow down and show the hows of cooking, and this has been our approach both in the new television series and in this book. I am frankly delighted with the results and I have thoroughly enjoyed being a part of the whole affair. In addition, I have picked up so many useful things myself!

There is so much to learn. And the more one learns the easier, faster, and more enjoyable cooking is. Besides, one takes pride in one's work. Just watching a practiced cook handle a knife is a learning experience—and we see a good deal of nifty knife-work in these shows. We are party to many little tricks that make cooking more efficient, like observing Amy Ferguson-Ota scoop out the seeds and ribs of a tomato quarter before she juliennes, to make really neat strips. Why didn't I think of doing that before? Alice Waters rubs a naked garlic clove over the tines of a fork facing down for a quick puree. How simple and effective! Again, it's watching someone establish logical work patterns like the Feniger–Milliken system for chopping and slicing vegetables—keep the scraps to the left and all the finished work to the right, or vice versa, then you sweep the ready vegetables into the pan, the scraps into the trash, and you've cleaned up your workplace. What a sensible way to operate!

Jeremiah Tower performs a clever string-truss for a chicken to be roasted or poached, and Amy Ferguson-Ota oils her hands before slicing and seeding spicy raw chiles—oiling hands first prevents irritation. When beating egg whites, Jacques Pépin whips them fast and hard for a few seconds to break them up before the serious beating begins. I used his system in a demonstration just the other day (giving him credit, of course), and had beautiful stiff, shining peaks.

We learn countless and wonderful ways with chocolate from Michel Richard. Jean-Louis Palladin shows us how to make an oven out of an ordinary fireplace, and Patrick Clark seasons a no-account fish with a horseradish crust and turns it into a gourmet's delight. Charlie Palmer illustrates the very useful process of searing steaks, while Robert Del Grande goes into the searing of big fresh sea scallops and also gives us two simple spicy salsas.

The recipes themselves are lessons in contemporary ingredients and combinations, making us aware of what is being cooked today and how food is presented by leading chefs around the country. In spite of their being given to us by professionals, the recipes here are all written expressly for the average serious home cook. Although few of us are equipped to arrange a series of individual dinner plates with the infinite artistry of a restaurant chef and staff, we observe in detail as the arrangement is made. Thus we gather ideas and may adapt them from plates to serving platters if we wish. If we forget how and what, the color photographs accompanying the recipes will remind us.

Here we are concentrating on individual chefs, but in the days of Escoffier, chefs were on the whole anonymous except for the great master himself. Other names still survive from those distant days, like Carême, Alexander Dumaine, Louis Diat, Henri Soulé—and almost to a man, they are French. But in this country, it was the restaurant or hotel, not the chef, that was remembered—Delmonico's, The Palm Court, The Parker House, The Palace in San Francisco. If the chef were known he was certainly a French or Swiss "he," never a "she."

In contrast, all sixteen of the chefs whose recipes appear in this book are nationally recognized. Ten of the sixteen are American, and five of those ten are women. Today, in the 1990s, the culinary arts have become a respected profession, and many of our chefs have university degrees. It is even possible to study for a master's degree in gastronomy. And about time, I say.

The joyful passion that the chefs showed for their chosen profession was what especially impressed me during our television tapings. Every one of our cooks adores and is utterly dedicated to the art, and takes tremendous pride both in its execution and in its teaching. They have a good time, and it shows. Before we began, we said to each of them, "We don't want show-off cooking like how to cut up a chicken in eleven seconds. We want real teaching. Consider your audience to be your apprentices, and really show us how you do things." As Jacques Pépin remarked, "We have cut up onions, rolled out pastry, and fluted mushrooms for so many years it's automatic. We forget we had to learn how, too, when we began." What a pleasure it is to watch the experts at work.

The reason I was attracted to the field myself, when we lived in France, was that aspect of pride, joy, and dedication that I found among the chefs with whom I learned—a dish to be done in the best possible way, however intricate its preparation, however long it took to achieve perfection of taste and presentation. Chef Patrick Clark had that same reaction when he apprenticed in France. "It was a total revelation for me," he says. He, and all of our group of chefs, have been leaders in bringing that spirit of dedication as well as a camaraderie here to us in this country. They all know, respect, and enjoy each other.

The art of cooking is indeed a noble hobby, and a fully satisfying profession. I've never run into a serious cook or chef of any age who didn't say: "Every day I learn something new!" That point of view turns home cooking and the pleasures of the table into a wonderful adventure.

—Julia Child
Cambridge, Massachusetts
May 1993

Acknowledgments

Geoffrey Drummond, producer of A La Carte Communications, bears the ultimate responsibility for *Cooking with Master Chefs*—the television series and the book. It was his idea in the first place, and it was he, with his assistant producer, Susie Heller, who gathered together and made all the arrangements for the chef participants. It was his wonderfully patient and talented director, Bruce Franchini, who made it all possible on the television screen—Bruce has had wide television experience and he knows food. The agile photographers who illustrated this book also get great praise from me; working often in the heat of battle they fought for the important angles, the crucial points, and essential closeups that bring the written word to life. It is that serious attention to detail that is impressive, and like our chefs, our television crew and photographers take such obvious joy and pride in their work. What a pleasure and privilege it has been for me to work with this team of professionals, and we've had a good time together.

It is an immense privilege, too, that I am with Alfred A. Knopf, Inc., who have been my publishers since 1961, starting with my first book, *Mastering the Art of French Cooking.* I remember my husband, Paul, being so delighted that it was Knopf. "They do such a beautiful job," he said happily. "They take pride in the printing, and in the design of the book. They care." They do, indeed, but it is not only the printing, it is the whole production and marketing aspect as well. I know how fortunate I have been all during my book career. But I also know so well that there would be nothing at all were it not for my editor, Judith Jones. We have worked together for over thirty years. My trust in her advice and judgment is absolute, and my gratitude profound.

Deepest and special thanks go to my friend and colleague, Nancy Verde Barr, "Without whom…" We first met while I was doing a fund-raising cooking demonstration some years ago for Planned Parenthood in Providence, Rhode Island. She appeared as a young volunteer from that organization, to help us out with buying, arranging, cooking, and so forth. She was wonderful in every way and we all said, "Let's hang on to her!" And we did, and we have all been together these many years—doing television series, book tours, demonstrations. Nancy is a teacher and cookbook writer herself, her first book (with Judith Jones) being *We Called It Macaroni.* When I found, while working on this book, that I'd never survive and get all the writing done on schedule by myself, I called for help, and Nancy came. We spent hours glued to the set, taking down every chefly word on our twin laptops, and she helped with the writing, and the chefs' biographies, and the reediting, and the proofing. We work well together, and my thanks are infinite.

Many thanks are certainly due to the home team and Stephanie Hersh, able cook, pastry chef, and assistant, who keeps everything humming. Kathleen Anino tested breads, cookies, and truffles, Alsatian stews, chocolate domes, and the like—making timely comments and suggestions—my thanks for her work so ably done.

A cookbook without a noteworthy index is both unthinkable and unusable—by good fortune Pat Kelly, member of The Culinary Historians of New England, who also indexed *The Way to Cook,* has also done her usual intelligent job for us here.

COOKING
WITH MASTER
CHEFS

Charles Palmer

Aureole, New York

Chef Charlie Palmer examining the beef with Marc Sarrazin of the DeBragga & Spitler wholesale meat market in the meat-packing district of Manhattan.

Charles Palmer may not have known what he wanted to do when he was growing up on a dairy farm and playing linebacker in the Chenango Valley in upstate New York, but he was very much in training for a successful career in professional kitchens. He learned to value real food at its farm source, and when he opened his restaurants—Aureole, Chef's Cuisiniers Club, and Periyali, in New York City—he built his own smokehouse, became a partner in a duck farm, and set up a network of small farmers who provide his restaurants with 70 percent of the produce and staples used. Chef Charlie feels that this intimate contact is essential to bringing his customers the very best. "Restaurants have the opportunity to have a big influence on producers. Farming in America has changed; what really changed it was the demand from food professionals who wanted better produce."

And the football? The strapping six-foot-four Palmer said that it helped him establish an extremely efficient kitchen. He says that the kitchen is like a football game: "It's a total team thing. If there's a weak link, it just won't work." He also finds that every night in the kitchen is like a new game, with all the adrenaline that makes you play your best regardless of what disaster might have happened the night before. According to restaurant critics, he's having a winning season.

Chef Charlie began cooking at fourteen in a home economics class and part-time in the kitchen of a local inn. It was love at first sight, and when he was sixteen he was put in charge of the inn's kitchen following the abrupt departure of the chef. At eighteen, he enrolled in the Culinary Institute of America in Hyde Park, New York, and became immediately enamored of formal French cuisine under the tutelage of classically trained European chefs. Realizing how much there was to know, Chef Charlie established a routine of traveling regularly to Europe and throughout the United States. At first, he would go wherever the cheapest airfare would take him; he visited restaurants, met with chefs, and whenever he could he spent as much time as possible in the various kitchens.

With a firm foundation in classical training and good work experience, Chef Charlie, now thirty-three, has brought into being his personal vision of great contemporary restaurants with relaxed atmosphere, excellent service, and highly creative food. Palmer doesn't believe in culinary hijinks but he loves an element of surprise: "I like to shock people—especially with dessert. To start with a simple theme and then do something shocking. If you really know the classics, then you can vary as you like."

The recipes that Chef Charlie made for us, such as the warm chocolate cakes with their hint of tarragon and jauntily placed tuiles, the pan-seared venison steaks with fruity dried cherry sauce, and the "sandwiches" of oven-crisped potatoes with suspended sprigs of herbs are good examples of this talented young chef's expertise.

Pepper-Seared Venison Steaks with Pinot Noir and Sun-Dried Cherries

Chef Charlie grew up in a family of hunters in upstate New York, so his expertise with wild game came easily. These succulent pepper-seared venison steaks with their pleasantly tart/fruity sauce of sun-dried cherries and Pinot Noir wine are a perfect marriage of good rich flavors. People are eating more venison today, says he, because most venison today is farm raised and tender, needing no marinade. It is lean meat, too, a fact that appeals to many of the calorie conscious.

Farm-raised venison looks and tastes much like beef, and you may use the same recipe for beef tenderloin or loin of lamb. Chef Charlie serves his venison steaks with creamy molded flans of butternut squash and almost paper-thin slices of oven-crisped herbed potatoes.

Venison Steaks (continued)

INGREDIENTS FOR 6 SERVINGS

For the venison steaks

*6 center-cut steaks of venison
(5-ounce steaks 1-½ inches
thick from the top loin)*

*3 tablespoons cracked black
peppercorns*

Kosher salt

3 tablespoons corn oil

For the sauce

3 tablespoons minced shallots

*1 cup red wine (Chef Charlie
uses Pinot Noir)*

¾ cup strong chicken stock

*⅓ cup sun-dried cherries
(soaked in hot water until
plump)*

*9 sprigs flat-leafed parsley,
stemmed and coarsely
chopped*

6 tablespoons unsalted butter

SPECIAL EQUIPMENT SUGGESTED

*A meat pounder or the side of
a bottle, or a heavy flat-
bottomed saucepan*

A heavy 10-inch frying pan

Preparing the Venison: Pat the venison steaks dry if necessary. Coat each side evenly with a good amount of pepper and a good pinch of salt. Then take a meat pounder or heavy pan and flatten the steaks to a thickness of ¾ inch, thus embedding the crust of pepper and salt.

Cooking the Venison—5 minutes: Set the skillet over high heat, film the pan with oil, and when beginning to smoke add the steaks, a few at a time so as not to crowd the pan. Sear for 2 to 3 minutes on one side, until brown and crusty. Turn the steaks over and sear for another 2 minutes. Press the meat with your finger: they should feel rare—between squashy and firm. Remove from the pan, repeat with remaining steaks, and keep in a warm place.

Making the Sauce: Pour the excess oil from the pan and place back on the heat. Add the minced shallots and sauté, stirring with a wooden spatula to bring up the drippings. Add the wine, chicken stock, drained soaked cherries, and chopped parsley: boil until the liquid has reduced by half.

Add the butter and any juices that have exuded from the venison. Let boil to thicken and blend flavors. Place the steaks back in the pan, and basting them with the sauce, simmer slowly for 1 minute or so to reheat the meat and bring it up to medium rare—but not to overcook it.

Serving Pepper-Seared Venison Steaks: Arrange the steaks on a plate and spoon the sauce over them. Serve immediately.

Herb Potato Maximes

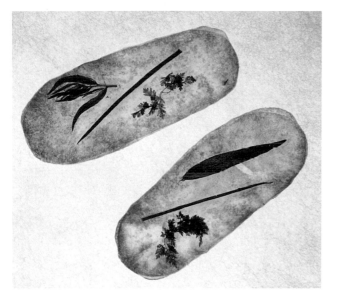

The most divine of big buttery potato chips, these are very thin long slices of potato sandwiched together with herb sprigs tucked inside and baked in the oven. Chef Charlie says he got the idea for them at Maxim's in Paris. Two apiece are never enough, so here are directions for three in our dinner party for six.

INGREDIENTS FOR 6 SERVINGS (18 PIECES)

1 stick (4 ounces) butter, clarified (see page 68)
20 fresh chives, the 1-½-inch points only
20 tarragon leaves
20 tiny chervil sprigs
2 unblemished evenly formed oval baking potatoes about 5 inches long
Salt

SPECIAL EQUIPMENT SUGGESTED

1 or 2 no-stick baking sheets
A pastry brush
A mandoline or other vegetable slicer

Preliminaries: Preheat the oven to 350° F and place the rack in the upper third level. Liberally brush a baking sheet with clarified butter. Pick the herbs into individual leaves or sprigs and set beside you.

Preparing the Potatoes: Peel the potatoes, trim into neat ovals, and slice the long side to flatten. Rinse in cold water and dry in a paper towel. Using a vegetable slicer, slice one potato paper-thin, getting 18 to 20 even oval pieces. Working quickly from now on so that the potatoes will not discolor, lay the slices closely together (but not touching) on the buttered baking sheet. Immediately brush with butter. Rapidly lay one piece of each herb free-form on each slice, keeping a small border clear around the edges.

Assembling the Potatoes: Always working quickly, slice the second potato the same way as the first. This time, dry the slices slightly and lay one slice evenly over each of the herb-topped slices. Once they are all arranged, press each one firmly to seal together and generously brush with the remaining clarified butter. Season lightly with salt.

Baking the Potatoes—10 minutes: Bake in the preheated oven for approximately 5 minutes. Turn the tray halfway around and bake another 4 to 5 minutes, until the potatoes are golden brown. Remove, drain on paper towels, and cool.

Serving Herb Potato Maximes: Serve at room temperature—they keep nicely for several hours.

Butternut Squash Timbales

A tender custard of pureed winter squash makes an attractive contrast to the robust flavors and texture of the peppered venison steaks. This is the general formula to use for making timbales of other puréed or minced vegetables, such as mushrooms, onions, broccoli, spinach, and so forth.

INGREDIENTS FOR 6 SERVINGS

3 cups peeled and seeded butternut squash, coarsely cut

Salt

½ cup heavy cream

3 "large" eggs

3 egg yolks

Several grinds of pepper

1 tablespoon softened unsalted butter

SPECIAL EQUIPMENT SUGGESTED

An electric blender

6 ramekins about 2-½ by 5 inches (⅔ cup capacity)

A baking pan to hold the ramekins

Preparing the Squash: Put the squash in a saucepan with ¼ teaspoon salt and barely enough water to cover. Bring to the boil, cover, and boil over moderately high heat for 10 minutes or more, until the squash is perfectly tender. Drain out the cooking water and, to evaporate excess moisture, toss the squash over moderate heat for several minutes, until it just begins to stick to the bottom of the pan.

Preparing the Custard Mixture: Puree the cream, eggs, and yolks in the blender. Add the cooked squash, salt and pepper to taste, and puree until smooth. Correct seasoning.

Baking the Timbales—20 minutes: Butter the ramekins, divide the squash custard among them, and arrange in the baking pan.

Ahead-of-Time Note: May be prepared several hours in advance to this point. Cover and refrigerate.

Preheat the oven to 325° F half an hour before baking and place the rack in the lower middle level. Bring a kettle of water to the boil. When the oven is ready, pour an inch of boiling water around the ramekins and set them in the oven. Bake for about 20 minutes, until a paring knife inserted into the center of each timbale comes out clean.

Serving Butternut Squash Timbales: Remove the ramekins from the pan of water and let settle for 5 minutes. Unmold onto warm plates, to accompany the venison steaks.

COOK'S NOTES

Chocolate Tarragon Dessert

Chef Charlie's Aureole is known for its spectacular desserts, and this is typical Palmer—handsome and unusual to look at—yet absolute heaven to eat. Meltingly warm chocolate cupcake mousses with an unusual hint of tarragon are decorated with egg-shaped dollops of whipped cream and tapering triangles of crisp chocolate wafers.

Chef Charlie got the idea for this dessert from a piece of candy, a chocolate ganache with essence of tarragon, that he ate at Witamer's in Brussels. He found that the tarragon gave a subtle but delicious flavor that he has re-created in this dessert.

Be sure to make your decorative elements for the cakes ahead, so that they will be ready when you assemble the dessert.

The Cupcake Mousses:

Preliminaries: Preheat the oven to 375° F and set the rack in the lower middle level. Butter the rings and cookie sheet or the ramekins.

Melting the Chocolate: In the bottom of the double boiler, bring 2 inches of water to the simmer, and maintain at just below the simmer. Place the bowl on top, and add the chocolate. Let melt slowly, occasionally stirring with a spoon, then remove from heat and blend in the butter. Set aside. (For more details about melting chocolate, see page 61.)

Preparing the Batter: Turn the egg yolks and ½ cup sugar into the second bowl; set over the barely simmering water and whisk until the mixture is just warm to your finger. Transfer to the mixer and whip about 5 minutes, until the eggs are pale yellow and fluffy. Turn off the mixer and add the tarragon; scrape down the sides of the bowl. Turn the mixer to low, and slowly pour in the melted chocolate, mixing only until blended.

Whipping the Egg Whites: In a very clean bowl, whip the egg whites to soft peaks, then slowly add the remaining sugar and continue whipping until the whites are stiff. (For more about beating egg whites, see page 134.)

Folding in the Egg Whites: Using a spatula, stir ⅓ of the whites into the chocolate mixture to lighten it. Rapidly and lightly fold in the rest—do not over-fold—a few random streaks of white are permitted.

INGREDIENTS FOR 6 TO 8 SERVINGS

For the batter
7 tablespoons unsalted butter at room temperature, plus 2 to 3 tablespoons for rings and cookie sheet (1-¾ sticks)
4 ounces semisweet chocolate
4 "large" eggs, separated
1 cup sugar
½ ounce fresh tarragon leaves, finely chopped (about 1-½ tablespoons)

(continued)

Chocolate Tarragon Dessert (continued)

For decoration

1 cup heavy cream, quite stiffly beaten

12 chocolate tuiles (see page 10)

About ½ cup chocolate sauce (see page 7)

About ¼ cup cocoa powder

SPECIAL EQUIPMENT SUGGESTED

6 small baking rings (about 2-½ by 2 inches) set on a cookie sheet, or individual ceramic ramekins

Chocolate-melting setup: an 8-inch saucepan with a close-fitting 12-inch stainless steel bowl set on it

A second stainless steel bowl, of a size to fit into the saucepan

A tabletop electric mixer with whisk attachment

For decoration

A soup spoon set in a pitcher of very hot water

A plastic squeeze bottle with pointed spout (optional)

A tea strainer to dust cocoa powder

Baking the Cakes—10 minutes: Spoon the batter into the rings or ramekins, and bake in the lower middle level of the preheated oven for about 10 minutes, until the top begins to crack open.

Unmolding the Cakes: Remove from the oven—this dessert is to be served warm. They must have a minimum of 2 to 3 minutes to set before unmolding but will stay warm for 20 minutes or so set on the opened door of the turned-off oven.

Ahead-of-Time Note: May be reheated for a moment in the oven to warm through, but the sooner you serve them the better.

Serving: Chef Charlie runs a small knife around the inside of the rings or ramekins and unmolds the desserts in the center of his dessert plates. Then, dipping the soup spoon into very hot water, he revolves the spoon in the whipped cream to form a neat shiny egg shape which he places at one side of the dessert. Dipping his spoon again into the hot water, he

deposits another egg of cream on top. Using the cream as an anchor, he tucks the large end of a tuile under each. He has decanted his chocolate sauce into his squeeze bottle, and squiggles chocolate around the structure (or one could dribble the sauce off the end of a spoon), and he finishes with a dusting of cocoa powder. He serves his masterpiece at once, while the chocolate is still warm.

Chocolate Tuiles
Thin Chocolate Sugar Wafers

Tuiles are sugar cookies that get bent out of shape. They are wonderfully useful to know how to make because they can turn even the humblest dessert into something elegant.

Preliminaries: Preheat the oven to 300° F.

Preparing the Batter: Whip the butter and honey in the machine of your choice, scraping down the sides of the container as necessary. Sieve the flour, sugar, and cocoa into a bowl. Then, with the machine running, gradually blend the flour mixture into the butter and honey. When fully incorporated, slowly pour in the egg whites. Whip for several minutes, until very smooth.

Forming the Tuiles into Long Triangles: Place the template near the corner of one of the cookie sheets. Using a spatula (preferably the offset kind because it's easier), spread a spoonful of the batter over the template. Lift

INGREDIENTS FOR 2 CUPS OF BATTER OR APPROXIMATELY 7 DOZEN TRIANGLE COOKIES, 6 BY 1-½" (HOME COOKS COULD FREEZE HALF THE DOUGH OR HALF THE BAKED COOKIES)

1 stick (4 ounces) unsalted butter
¼ cup honey
¾ cup all-purpose flour
1 cup confectioners' sugar
¼ cup cocoa powder
2 "large" egg whites (¼ cup)

OTHER USES FOR TUILE DOUGH

Chef Charlie's tuiles were flavored with chocolate, but the same technique can be used for a plain dough using the following ingredients:

3-½ tablespoons soft butter
½ cup sugar
2 "large" egg whites
5 tablespoons plain cake flour
⅓ cup ground blanched almonds (see page 34)
¼ teaspoon almond extract
¼ teaspoon vanilla extract
Topping: ½ cup sliced almonds

What makes tuiles especially fun to prepare is the fact that you can form them into any shape you like, either by tracing an outline on a cookie sheet that has been buttered and floured and then free-forming the batter or by making a cutout in a piece of cardboard or light plastic. Tuiles can be made into edible dessert cups by draping the hot dough over an upturned teacup or pressing it inside the cup. Let crisp—which happens almost immediately—and remove.

off the template and, leaving a space of 1 inch, form another triangle, et cetera. (Bake one pan while preparing another.)

Baking the Tuiles—8 minutes: Set the pan on the middle level rack in the preheated oven and bake until the cookies have lost their shiny gloss, meaning they are done—7 to 8 minutes.

Forming the Baked Tuiles: Remove from the oven and let cool on the cookie sheet for about 25 seconds to firm up just enough for lifting them off with a spatula. With your clean spatula, carefully dislodge a tuile and drape it crosswise over the rolling pin or bottle, where it will quickly crisp into the curved shape of a roof tile or "tuile." Since they cool and crisp in just a few seconds, you must work fast: you will probably have to reheat the sheet briefly in the oven several times to soften them for shaping.

Ahead-of-Time Note: Baked tuiles lose their crispness in damp weather, and they do not keep well anyway. However, they will be fine for several hours in a warming oven, or they may be frozen. The uncooked dough may be frozen for months.

COOK'S NOTES

Mary Sue Milliken and Susan Feniger

City Café and Border Grill, Santa Monica

Susan Feniger and Mary Sue Milliken enjoying the spicy aromas.

When the California Restaurant Writers Association chose their 1988 chef of the year, the award went to the exciting team of Susan Feniger and Mary Sue Milliken. The honor was a recognition of two women whose careers seemed destined to merge.

They began cooking as high school students in the Midwest; Mary Sue in a Michigan pizza parlor and Susan in a Toledo cafeteria. Mary Sue then pursued the Chef's Program at the Washburne Trade School and apprenticed at the Conrad Hilton kitchens in Chicago. Susan headed to California and worked in a faculty dining room while studying business and economics; she then attended the Culinary Institute of America. The young chefs met after Mary Sue convinced Jovan Treboyevic to accept her as the first female to his staff at Chicago's Le Perroquet; Susan became the second.

While Mary Sue continued in Illinois, Susan found a position with Wolfgang Puck at Ma Maison in Los Angeles. They lost touch, but when Mary Sue left for a sabbatical at the restaurant Olympe in Paris, and Susan headed for L'Oasis on the French Riviera, they coincidentally met in Paris and vowed one day they'd work together.

Chef Susan returned to Ma Maison, but managed to find time to work in the mornings at the tiny City Café nearby. When she became a partner, Mary Sue joined her, thus beginning a partnership that was instantly acclaimed for its originality and individuality. They opened the larger City with an expanded menu that featured dishes based on Mary Sue's travels to Thailand and Susan's culinary explorations in India. Extensive travels in Mexico led to the opening of a second restaurant, the Border Grill in Santa Monica. This energetic team gives us examples here of the eclectic cuisine that has made them two of the most successful chefs in contemporary cooking.

Orange Dal with Ginger and Garlic

This spicy lentil dish could be the vegetable to go with broiled or grilled chicken, or with lamb, or it could be a light first course. If you use water or vegetable broth rather than chicken broth, and combine rice with the lentils to make a complete protein, you can serve the dish as a complete vegetarian lunch, adding perhaps some crisp-fried onions and a topping of yogurt. Dal is any legume such as the lentil. The orange lentils they use are lighter and sweeter than darker lentils, as well as being smaller and more fragile. Most supermarkets carry them, as do health food stores.

Preparing the Dal: Spread the dal (orange lentils) on a cookie sheet and pick out any stones or clumps of dirt. Place them in a large bowl and wash under cold running water until the water runs clear, about 10 minutes. Drain in the colander or sieve.

Cooking the Dal: Set the saucepan over moderate heat, add the butter, and when bubbling stir in the cumin seeds; sauté, stirring for several minutes, until the seeds have browned lightly. Stir in the onions, salt, and pepper. Sauté until golden brown, then add the garlic and ginger and continue sautéing for 2 to 3 minutes. Finally, stir in the washed dal and the stock; bring to the simmer, cover, and cook 20 to 30 minutes until tender. Taste, correct seasoning, fold in the chopped cilantro, and serve.

Ahead-of-Time Note: Cooked dal may be kept under refrigeration for 2 to 3 days. Reheat over hot water before serving.

INGREDIENTS FOR 6 SERVINGS

2 cups dal (orange lentils)

For the background flavors
2 tablespoons clarified butter (see page 68)
2 tablespoons cumin seeds
2 large onions, finely diced (3 cups)
1 teaspoon salt
1 teaspoon white pepper
2 tablespoons pureed garlic
2 tablespoons freshly grated ginger
2-½ cups chicken stock, vegetable broth, or water

For the garnish
1 bunch chopped cilantro, or to your taste

SPECIAL EQUIPMENT SUGGESTED

A fine-holed colander or fine-meshed sieve
A 2- to 2-½-quart heavy-bottomed saucepan

Curry Popcorn

Chefs Mary Sue and Susan keep huge bowls of this bright orange popcorn at the bar in their restaurant at all times. Adjust the seasoning to your own taste, they advise, since it is definitely spicy.

INGREDIENTS FOR 3 QUARTS

½ teaspoon, or to your taste,
   red pepper flakes
1 teaspoon ground cumin
½ teaspoon turmeric
1 teaspoon cracked black
   peppercorns
1 teaspoon salt
¼ cup vegetable oil
½ cup unpopped popcorn

SPECIAL EQUIPMENT SUGGESTED

A heavy-duty saucepan or
   casserole with tight-fitting
   cover

Measure the spices onto a plate and place near the stove. To test for the right heat, pour the oil into the saucepan and add a single kernel of popcorn. Turn the heat to high, and cover the pan. When the kernel pops, quickly pour in the rest and cover the pan again. When the corn really starts popping, hold your breath and rapidly toss in the spices and cover the pan—don't breath in the spice fumes, they'll burn your throat at this point. Keep shaking the covered pan until the popping stops.

KEEPING THE WORKPLACE NEAT

Mary Sue Milliken and Susan Feniger are fast, neat workers, and experts with the knife, as professionals must be. An excellent habit to cultivate when chopping and slicing, for instance, is to keep all the scraps to the left and all your work to the right. As an example, when slicing onions peel them and push the peels to your left, then slice them and push the slices to your right. When you're through, you simply sweep the peels into the trash, the slices into a bowl, and—presto—your counter is clean.

A Curry of Spinach and Eggplant

Here is another of Chefs Mary Sue and Susan's vegetarian recipes that are happy in the role of first course, or the main course for a lunch, or an important dinner side dish. Of especial interest is the eggplant, both as a fine illustration of how to sauté successfully with minimum oil consumption and as a lesson in making your own curry powder.

Preparing the Eggplant: Wash the eggplant, cut off and discard the green cap, and cut the purple part lengthwise into even ½-inch slices. Cut the slices into ½-inch strips, and the strips into ½-inch dice. Toss in a colander with the coarse salt, and let drain for 20 minutes. (For more about eggplant, see page 17.)

Preparing the Mustard Seeds: Meanwhile, measure the mustard seeds into the dry 6-inch frying pan and sauté briefly over moderate heat, until they turn gray and start popping—the heat brings out their aroma. Set aside.

Sautéing the Eggplant: When the eggplant has drained its 20 minutes, dry it thoroughly in a paper towel, so that it will sauté rather than steam. Pour 4 tablespoons of the clarified butter into the 12-inch frying pan and

INGREDIENTS FOR 4 TO 6 SERVINGS

1 large, firm, shiny eggplant (about 1-½ pounds)
1-½ teaspoons coarse salt
2 tablespoons black or yellow mustard seeds
6 tablespoons clarified butter (see page 68)

(continued)

Spinach and Eggplant Curry (continued)

For the curry

1 large onion, diced (1-½ cups)

½ teaspoon salt

2 tablespoons chopped garlic (3 to 4 large cloves)

2 tablespoons freshly grated ginger (see page 71)

3 teaspoons ground cumin

½ teaspoon ground coriander

½ teaspoon ground cardamom

½ teaspoon turmeric

¼ teaspoon ground cloves

½ teaspoon cayenne pepper

2 tomatoes, peeled, seeded, and diced

1 cup water

1 tablespoon palm sugar (or light brown sugar)

For the finish

2 bunches (20 ounces) fresh spinach, washed, stemmed, and cut into 2-inch slices

SPECIAL EQUIPMENT SUGGESTED

A 6-inch frying pan
A 12-inch frying pan
A 10-inch saucepan

set over moderately high heat. When the butter is hot, add the eggplant and sauté for several minutes, tossing and turning; regulate the heat so that the eggplant is no darker than a nice golden brown. When soft, turn it into a bowl and toss with the mustard seeds.

Preparing the Curry: Heat the remaining butter in the 10-inch saucepan over moderately high heat. Stir in the onions and salt and sauté, stirring frequently, until the onions are golden and soft. Add garlic and ginger, cook just a few seconds, until their aromas are released, then stir in all of the spices listed. Cook an additional minute, stirring con-stantly to blend spices and pre-

vent them from scorching. Stir in the tomatoes, water, and sugar. Turn the heat to high and bring to the boil.

Ahead-of-Time Note: You could stop at this point. Cover and refrigerate everything, and bring to the boil several hours later.

Finishing the Dish: Add the spinach, bring back to the boil, then stir in the eggplant. When the eggplant is heated through, in about a minute, the dish is ready to serve.

Pickled Tomatoes

Packed into attractive jars, these potent sweet-and-spicy tomatoes make lovely Christmas presents or house gifts. Our chefs serve small ramekins of this Indian relish with vegetarian platters at their restaurant; it is equally at home with egg and meat dishes.

Preparing the Ingredients to Be Pickled: Peel the tomatoes, cut them into 6 wedges, and turn them into the big bowl. Trim off the root ends and withered leaves and cut the scallions into wide slanting slices. If you like your chiles hot, simply wash them and cut into very thin crosswise slices. For a milder effect, quarter them lengthwise, scoop out the seeds, then slice them. Set aside.

Preparing the Pickling Medium: Bring the vinegar to the boil in one of the saucepans, add the sugar and salt, and simmer a moment, swirling the pan, until salt and sugar are dissolved. Set aside.

Preparing the Spices, and Finishing the Pickling: Measure the spices onto the plate. Pour the oil into the second saucepan, and set over moderate heat until almost smoking. Add the spices and cook, stirring constantly with the wooden spoon, until the aromas are released—about 2 minutes. Remove from heat and stir in the vinegar mixture. Immediately pour over the reserved tomatoes—a hot marinade penetrates the ingredients more effectively than a cold one. Mix well, cover with plastic wrap, and refrigerate for at least 3 days.

Ahead-of-Time Note: The tomatoes will keep a good month—if not consumed in a day or two, transfer to a screw-cap jar.

EGGPLANT THE FENIGER-MILLIKEN WAY

Eggplant is a handsome vegetable indeed, with its green cap and its purple skin. Look over every one with care when buying, to be sure it feels taut with no soft spots and that the skin is shiny. Dull skin and soft flesh mean bitter taste. Eggplants do have some natural bitterness, however, and the flesh contains moisture.

When you are baking or steaming whole eggplants, this presents no problems, but when you are baking slices or sautéing pieces you salt the eggplant first; this will remove any bitterness and draw out the water at the same time. Toss the eggplant in a colander with about 1 teaspoon of coarse salt per pound of eggplant—coarse salt dissolves slowly and is more efficient in drawing out moisture. Let the eggplant drain for 20 minutes. Then dry thoroughly in a towel—if the eggplant is wet, and you plan to sauté, it will absorb too much of the cooking oil.

INGREDIENTS FOR 3 CUPS

For the ingredients to be pickled
1-½ pounds tomatoes
2 bunches scallions (white and green)
3 to 5 serrano chiles, with seeds

For the pickling medium
¾ cup white vinegar
¼ cup brown sugar
1 tablespoon coarse salt

For the spices
2 tablespoons finely sliced fresh ginger
2 tablespoons pureed garlic
1 tablespoon black or yellow mustard seeds
1 tablespoon cracked black peppercorns
1 tablespoon ground cumin
2 teaspoons cayenne pepper
1 teaspoon turmeric
¾ cup olive oil

SPECIAL EQUIPMENT SUGGESTED

A large glass or stainless steel bowl
2 6-cup saucepans
A large flat plate
A long wooden spoon
A quart preserving jar

Lemon-Ginger Tea

Lemon-ginger tea—the very sound of it is refreshing, and especially so when served with spicy Thai and more often with Indian food.

INGREDIENTS FOR 1 QUART

1 quart water
The juice of 3 lemons
¾ pound fresh ginger, peeled and sliced very thin (more information is on page 71)
¼ cup honey
Thin slices of lemon and lime

SPECIAL EQUIPMENT SUGGESTED

A 2-quart saucepan
A fine-meshed sieve lined with washed cheesecloth
A handsome glass pitcher

Bring the water to the boil in the saucepan. Remove from heat, stir in the lemon juice and ginger, cover the pan and let steep for 20 minutes. Then stir in the honey, and strain through the cheesecloth-lined sieve into the pitcher. Chill thoroughly for several hours.

Serve in attractive ice-filled glasses, and decorate with the slices of lemon and lime.

THAI SEASONINGS

Chefs Mary Sue and Susan use some ingredients that may not be in supermarkets, depending on where you live. They can be found in oriental grocery stores.

Thai Fish Sauce: A rather mild sauce, a little salty, only faintly fishy, it includes dried anchovies, dried shrimp, and/or other dried fish. You can substitute a little soy sauce, either plain or diluted with water.

Palm Sugar: Made from coconut, palm sugar is milder than a light brown sugar, which can be substituted.

Kaffir Lime Leaves: They come in little packages in Thai markets, and exude a great bouquet. Substitute grated lime peel.

Thai Melon Salad

Several types of diced ripe melons on a platter, all dressed with a spicy Thai dressing—serve it as a first course or as part of a luncheon or a midday break. This is one of the dishes that inspired Chef Mary Sue on her trip to Bangkok, where melons grow abundantly. A good use for melons, too, remarks Chef Susan, who favors taking them out of the breakfast-only category. And a good use for the Thai dressing, which also goes beautifully on green beans, boiled potatoes, chicken salad, and so forth.

Preparing the Dressing: Pour the fish sauce or soy sauce into a mixing bowl along with the sugar. Either chop and add the Kaffir leaves, or scrape in the lime zest; pour in the lime juice, and stir the mixture to make sure the sugar dissolves completely. Grind the dried shrimp to a powder in the chopper, add the peanuts, and with several on-off pulses chop them roughly. Peel the garlic cloves, dice them finely with a very sharp knife, and stir into the dressing along with the dried shrimp and peanuts. Chop the cilantro and part of the stems and stir half into the dressing; reserve the rest to garnish the finished dish.

Ahead-of-Time Note: The dressing may be made 2 or 3 days in advance. Refrigerate in a covered jar.

Dicing the Melons: Cut a slice off the top and stem end of a cantaloupe or honey dew, and stand it on one end. Slice off the rind in strips, and continue shaving off hard white or unripe parts, until you come to the tender ripe flesh. Cut the melon in half lengthwise; remove the seeds and any strings. Cut the melon into neat ¾-inch horizontal slices, and cut the slices into neat ¾-inch dice. Reserve in a bowl. Continue with the next melon, reserving it in its own separate bowl. When you have diced the watermelon, carefully poke out as many seeds as you easily can and reserve the flesh in its own bowl. Cover all three bowls and chill.

Serving Thai Melon Salad: To serve, whisk up the dressing; if too thick, whisk in droplets of lime juice. Toss each melon with a spoonful of dressing, then arrange in alternating rows on the platter. Spoon the dressing over the melons in a stripe and garnish with cilantro. Serve chilled.

TO JUICE A LIME

Chef Susan always softens the limes by rolling and pressing them under the palm of her hand against her work surface. She cuts them in half crosswise, twists the tines of a fork into the flesh to break the membranes, then juices them.

INGREDIENTS FOR 6 SERVINGS

For the dressing

¼ cup Thai fish sauce (or 1 teaspoon soy sauce to taste)

2 tablespoons palm sugar (or light brown sugar)

1 tablespoon Kaffir lime leaves (or 1 teaspoon grated lime zest—see page 135)

¼ cup fresh lime juice (2 or 3 limes)

½ cup dried shrimp

½ cup unsalted roasted peanuts

3 large garlic cloves

A medium-sized bunch, or to taste, fresh cilantro

The melons

Assorted melons, such as cantaloupe, watermelon, and honeydew, to make about 6 cups in all

SPECIAL EQUIPMENT SUGGESTED

A chopper or grinder (electric blender or mini food processor)

3 bowls, one for each melon

A 10- by 14-inch serving platter

Emeril Lagasse

He's the quintessential New Orleans chef and he's from Fall River, Massachusetts. Emeril Lagasse was at the helm of the legendary Commander's Palace for seven and a half years before opening Emeril's in 1990—drawing crowds and amassing awards immediately. His second venture, NOLA, opened in 1992, and is already a huge success.

This energetic young chef traces his culinary passion to his youth in a New England seaside town where food was an important part of life with his Portuguese mother and French Canadian father. "I'd come home from school and say to my mother, 'Let's cook.'" Emeril turned down a music scholarship so he could pursue his first love at Johnson and Wales Culinary School. He honed his skills in Paris and Lyon and built his reputation at restaurants in New York, Boston, and Philadelphia. When Ella and Dick Brennan lured him to Commander's, he felt as though he'd returned to his roots. "When I closed my eyes, I felt that this was where I was born. The people, the culture, the music, the spice, the hospitality—it all felt like home."

He was substituting crabs and crawfish for clams and lobster under the tutelage of a dynamic mentor. "It was like magic when I met Ella." With her encouragement, he steeped himself in the region's culture, fished with the fishermen, dug crawfish in the Bayou, raised rabbit and quail, and absorbed the essence of this rich cuisine. "There is a tremendous amount of taste and an extraordinary melting pot of flavors from the Cajuns, Creoles, French, and Spanish."

Chef Emeril's book, *Emeril's* New *New Orleans Cooking,* is an exciting example of how he has updated the traditional cuisine with dishes that maintain the intensity of flavors but with a more modern preparation. He demonstrates his knowledge and expertise for us with a traditional spicy crab boil and a classic rich shrimp *étouffée.*

Shrimp Étouffée

Certainly one of the classic dishes of New Orleans is the *étouffée*, pronounced "ay-too-fay," a spicy rich brown stew of chicken, duck, or sausages, but most often in New Orleans it's an *étouffée* of their wonderfully fresh shrimp and crawfish. In addition to the perfect quality of the main ingredient, the key to any successful *étouffée* is the excellence of its base—its roux, which is fully described on page 26.

A Note on Gulf Shellfish: Emeril Lagasse, of course, has all the fresh shellfish of Louisiana to choose from, including fresh shrimp for his heady shellfish stock. Those of us in other parts of the country can certainly use his general techniques, adapting them to what we have. Live lobster, for instance, makes a wonderful *étouffée*, or best-quality frozen shrimp, when you can find it. Shelled fresh crawfish tails are bought by the bagful in New Orleans; frozen crawfish tails are also available and they can be very good. The recipe here follows Chef Emeril's for fresh shrimp *étouffée*, as he did it on television.

Preparing the Shrimp: Set aside 4 to 6 whole unpeeled shrimp for final decoration. Shell the rest of the shrimp as follows: Hold the body in one hand, grasp the head in the other and snap it back and off. Pinch the feet at the tail end and pull them off. Working from the underside of the shrimp, peel the shell from the body, removing the tail with it. (Reserve the heads, tails, and shells to make the shrimp stock on page 23.)

To remove the intestinal vein (the black or greenish vein that may or may not be visible along the curve of the back), lay the shrimp on its side on the counter and with a sharp knife make a long slit along the back. With the tip of the knife, scrape out and discard the vein. Rinse the shrimp one at a time under cold tap water.

Preparing the Sauce Base: Mix together the ingredients for the mirepoix. Heat the roux in the saucepan, stirring. Still stirring, and when very hot, slide in the mirepoix vegetables. Cook, stirring rather slowly, for 2 to 3 minutes over high heat, until the onions are translucent. Remove from heat, and vigorously beat in the beer, whisking until smooth. Return the pan to the burner and over moderately high heat add the bay leaves and whisk while gradually pouring in the stock. Continuing to whisk, add 1 tablespoon of the Creole seasoning, the hot pepper sauce, and the Worcestershire sauce; salt to taste. Simmer slowly for 20 minutes, and again correct seasoning.

INGREDIENTS FOR 4 TO 6 SERVINGS

For the shrimp
2 pounds (24) whole large shrimp in the shell (or headless shrimp in the shell)
1 tablespoon Creole seasoning (see page 27)

For the Creole mirepoix
1 medium-sized green bell pepper, diced
1 medium-sized onion, sliced
1 medium-sized celery stalk, sliced
3 medium-sized garlic cloves, minced

For the sauce
1 ½ cups dark roux (see page 26)

(continued)

Shrimp Étouffée (continued)

2 bottles (or 24 ounces)
    dark beer
3 bay leaves
2 cups shrimp stock (see
    opposite page)
2 tablespoons Creole seasoning
2 teaspoons hot pepper sauce
2 tablespoons Worcestershire
    sauce
Salt

For serving
4 to 5 cups steamed
    or boiled rice
3 or 4 green onions or
    scallions, finely sliced
2 to 3 teaspoons Creole
    seasoning

**SPECIAL EQUIPMENT
SUGGESTED**

A 3-quart saucepan, about 10
    inches wide and 4 inches
    high
A heavy whisk
Warmed dinner plates

Ahead-of-Time Note: The sauce may be made up to 3 days in advance; when cool, cover and refrigerate. Heat to bubbling before proceeding.

Adding the Shellfish: Sprinkle the shellfish with the remaining tablespoon of Creole seasoning; stir the shellfish, including those reserved for decoration, into the bubbling sauce, and simmer for 2 to 3 minutes, until the shrimp turn pink. Taste carefully for seasoning.

Serving Shrimp Étouffée: Spoon a portion of hot rice into the center of each warm dinner plate, and surround with a serving of shrimp and sauce. Place one of the reserved unpeeled shrimp decoratively on top of the rice and top it with a big spoonful of sauce. Scatter the green onions over both shrimp and rice, and sprinkle Creole seasoning over all, including a dusting at the edges of the plate.

SHRIMP STOCK

INGREDIENTS FOR ABOUT 2 QUARTS
1 quart shrimp heads and shells
1 medium-sized onion, peeled and roughly chopped
1 medium-sized carrot, peeled and roughly chopped
1 medium-sized celery stalk, roughly chopped
1 lemon, zested, halved, and juiced (all goes in the pot)
4 bay leaves
10 parsley sprigs (leaves and stems), roughly chopped
½ teaspoon each: dried basil, oregano, and thyme
24 whole black peppercorns
1 teaspoon salt
2 quarts water

Assemble all the ingredients listed in a stockpot. Bring to the boil over high heat. Reduce heat to low and simmer for 40 minutes. Strain, pressing hard to extract juices out of ingredients. Let cool uncovered, then cover and refrigerate or freeze.

Louisiana Boil

The steamy and colorful Louisiana boil is a meal fit for a king, or at least a small army. As soon as crabs and crawfish are in season together, from spring until the midsummer "hot of sun," Louisianans gather in backyards, at beaches, or on fairgrounds to share this traditional meal. It's a bountiful, utterly informal picnic-style feast.

The traditional boil always has potatoes, onions, corn on the cob, whole heads of garlic, and andouille sausage. Today, Louisianans add whatever else appeals to them—artichokes, asparagus, mushrooms, even hot dogs. Whatever you put in the pot will absorb the spiciness of the seasoned cooking broth. The proportions of vegetables and shellfish are not important, but the items that take the longest to boil go in first.

The boil is cooked on a "Louisiana rig," a common piece of equipment in any home in this Southern state. It's a low propane-fired stand that holds a very large and deep kettle—some as large as 30 gallons—with a sturdy removable basket insert and tight-fitting lid. Every southern hardware store sells this rig, but you can adapt your home equipment (see Chef Emeril's on page 20).

Louisiana Boil (continued)

INGREDIENTS FOR 8
SERVINGS, MORE OR LESS

These are very informal
amounts. Everyone should get
at least one of everything,
such as a small crab or a
potato, a handful of artichoke
leaves, or a piece of sausage.
The following list is an
example only; put in what
you want, or can find.

For the cooking stock
6 gallons water
1-½ to 2 cups salt (or to taste)
2 tablespoons black
*   peppercorns*
Seasonings (see page 27)
*   4 packages dry crab boil*
*   2 cups liquid crab boil*
*   2 tablespoons hot sauce*
*   2 tablespoons Creole*
*   seasoning*

For the vegetables and sausage
16 red-skinned (or new)
*   potatoes, 2-inch diameter*
4 large artichokes
4 or more ears of corn,
*   shucked and halved*
A 2-foot piece of andouille
*   sausage, or other spicy*
*   sausage, in lengths or links*
6 lemons, cut in half
4 medium-sized yellow onions,
*   peeled and quartered*

(continued)

Preparing the Cooking Stock: Set the kettle with its basket insert on the rig, pour in the water, and turn the heat on to high. Add the seasonings listed, cover the kettle, and bring to the boil. Taste the stock, and adjust the seasoning to be as salty and as spicy as you wish it to be.

Cooking the Vegetables and Sausage: With the cooking stock at the full boil, start by adding the vegetables that will take the longest to cook: the potatoes and the artichokes. Cover the pot, bring to the boil again, and cook for 5 minutes. Add the corn, the sausage, lemons, onions, garlic, asparagus, celery, and scallions to the pot. Cover the pot and boil again for 5 minutes.

Cooking the Crabs, Crawfish, and Shrimp: Taste the stock again for salt and spices. Add the crab, and set the crawfish on top. Tuck the ingredients down into the stock with the wooden paddle. Cover the kettle, and when the stock returns to the rolling boil add the shrimp and turn the flame off (if the crawfish boil any longer, they will be difficult to peel). Let steep for 5 to 30 minutes, depending on how spicy you like it—the longer it steeps, the stronger the seasoning will be.

Serving Louisiana Boil: Place bowls of melted butter on the table, bottles of cold beer and mineral water, and perhaps a pitcher of iced tea. Have plenty of paper towels handy. Knives and forks can be provided, but Louisianans use their fingers.

Lift out the basket and suspend it for a few seconds over the kettle while it drains. Then dramatically spill the steaming contents onto the table, and everyone digs in.

Note on Eating Crawfish: Louisianans can easily spot a Yankee: he's the one who can neither pronounce nor eat a crawfish. It's "craw," as in "saw," not "cray" as in "say." Southerners also call them "mud bugs," because crawfish dig their way out of the mud, leaving a mound of wet earth behind them. To eat a crawfish, "suck the head and pinch the tail," as it is locally described. Pick the crawfish up with your fingers and twist off the head; suck out its juices. Turn the tail feet side up; twist off the first little group of feet and, still from the under- or feet side, peel off the first ring of shell from around the body. You now have an exposed end of tail meat to grab onto. To do so, hold the flesh end of the tail to your mouth and feel the tail end of the meat through the shell with your fingers; pinch hard to break the flesh loose from the shell at the tail end, then draw the sweet tender meat out of the shell and into your mouth with your teeth.

COOK'S NOTES

....

....

....

....

....

....

....

....

4 *heads garlic, halved*
   horizontally
2-½ *pounds asparagus*
1 *bunch celery, well washed*
   and tops removed
24 *scallions, trimmed and cut*
   into 6-inch lengths

For the shellfish
(the following are Louisiana
choices; use what is available
in your area)
12 *live blue crabs*
5 *pounds live crawfish*
2 *pounds fresh whole shrimp*

For serving
Bowls of melted butter
Plenty of cold beer, mineral
   water, and iced tea

SPECIAL EQUIPMENT
SUGGESTED

The Louisiana rig (see page
   23) or alternative
A long wooden paddle for
   stirring
A dining table covered with
   brown paper or newspaper
Rolls of paper towels

Louisiana Roux

When Louisianans give you a recipe for bisque, *étouffée,* or gumbo, they always begin by saying, "First, you make a roux," the flour-based thickening agent. It is just assumed that you'll know how. Although the principle of fat and flour cooked together is the same as the classic French roux, the Louisiana technique is unique to this part of the country, and, in years gone by, the desirability of many a New Orleanian bride was judged by her ability to make a good roux.

The color of the roux depends on the length of time it cooks and will vary according to how it is used. Light or "blonde" roux are used for bisques and soups, medium roux for sauces and ragouts, and the traditional dark brown roux is the basis for *étouffées* and gumbos. The dark roux is not at all difficult to make; it just needs careful and continual attention so that it is a deep nutty walnut brown, with its characteristic nut flavor. The hasty and careless cook will not be watching its last minutes of cooking and will often let the roux burn to a bitter black.

Although Louisianans can buy a ready-made roux at the local grocery, or make a lazy roux by mixing flour and oil to a paste, spreading it on a roasting pan, and letting it brown overnight in a very slow oven, nothing compares in taste and quality to stood-over, hand-stirred, old-fashioned brown roux. Is it the care that goes into it? Or is it, as for Lidia Bastianich's splendid risotto, the constant stirring?

INGREDIENTS FOR 1-½ CUPS

½ cup fine fresh vegetable oil
1 cup all-purpose flour

SPECIAL EQUIPMENT SUGGESTED

A heavy saucepan, 10 inches wide and 4 inches deep
A whisk
A wooden spoon

Preparing the Roux: Pour the oil into the saucepan and set over moderate heat, allowing the oil to come slowly just to the smoking point. The oil must not burn, since that would not only ruin its fresh taste but make it bitter.

As soon as the smoking point is reached, pour in the flour and immediately start to whisk vigorously. The mixture will smooth out as you whisk, and when it has the consistency of wet

sand, change from whisk to wooden spoon. Stirring rather slowly and constantly, and reaching all over the bottom of the pan, continue cooking the roux over moderately high heat. It will gradually turn blonde (the color for soups and bisques), then medium brown (for ragouts and some sauces). Finally, after 25 to 30 minutes it will be the color of dark peanut butter or dark walnut. It should have a fine toasty-nutty smell.

Ahead-of-Time Note: Once the roux is made, it can be cooled and stored in the refrigerator in a covered container—Chef Emeril says it will keep perfectly up to 1 week.

LOUISIANA SEASONINGS

Big flavor is what Louisiana food is all about, and a number of seasonings are staples in Louisiana kitchens. Many of these are also available in supermarkets around the country, or from catalogs, and some you can make yourself.

Creole Mirepoix: An aromatic vegetable flavoring for soups, stews, and general cooking, classic French mirepoix is a combination of diced onions, celery, and carrots. Creole mirepoix eliminates the carrots, adding green pepper and garlic instead.

Crab Boil: Dry crab boil is a commercially prepared flavoring mixture of salt, lemon juice, peppercorns, bay leaves, cloves, thyme, and marjoram. Used by professionals and home cooks, it is packed in small mesh bags that are tossed as is into the cooking broth. Concentrated liquid crab boil is the essential oils of all of the above. Liquid and dry can be used interchangeably; Chef Emeril uses a combination.

Andouille Sausage: A coarse-ground, lean smoked pork that is highly spiced with garlic and Creole seasoning, this sausage is unique to Louisiana and used as a flavoring for many dishes.

Creole Seasoning: Emeril Lagasse's homemade blend is the Louisiana standard used in *étouffées*, gumbos, crab boils, and in any dish where you want that authentic Louisiana taste. This salt-based spice mixture will keep for months in an airtight container.

INGREDIENTS FOR ⅔ CUP
2 tablespoons salt
2-½ tablespoons paprika
2 tablespoons garlic powder
1 tablespoon dried oregano
1 tablespoon cayenne pepper
1 tablespoon black pepper
1 tablespoon onion powder
1 tablespoon dried thyme

Mix all the ingredients together and store in an airtight container.

Hot Sauce: Louisiana hot pepper sauces are sold in bottles everywhere around the country. They vary in their degree of "heat," and their secret flavorings, but they are most often based on a combination of peppers and vinegar. Hot sauces are added to a dish while it is cooking as well as at the table, to give it a little fire.

André Soltner

André Soltner enjoying his Alsatian bacheofe *with his wife, Simone (left), and his niece Valerie (right).*

Chef André Soltner has a list of awards longer than his towering toque is high, but he doesn't seem impressed—although he does smile when talking of his induction into the Hall of Fame of Hunter Mountain skiers. This is an annual ski race in which more than two dozen well-known chefs tackle the Catskill slopes in full chef's regalia. The event has been going on since 1975 and André, who grew up on skis in the Vosges mountains of Alsace, has never missed a race.

"Eating and drinking hold body and soul together," according to an old Alsatian saying, and it's not surprising that young André should have chosen the restaurant profession. His part of Alsace was rich in ancient gastronomic culture, and the pleasures of the table, however modest, were enthusiastically pursued by everyone in the region. Being a cook was not, however, in his immediate consideration since he came from a family of woodworkers, and he thought of joining his father and brother as a cabinetmaker. His mother discouraged him, however, saying there were already enough of them in the family. "I told her that was all right with me because I'd just as soon be a chef."

He began his apprenticeship in March of 1948 at the Hôtel du Park in Mulhouse, near his home. By the time he was twenty-seven he was directing a brigade of seventeen chefs at Chez Hansi in Paris, and stacking up the first of a lifetime of awards and distinctions. In 1961, André Surmain wanted a French chef for the restaurant Lutèce in New York, and had heard of a certain young Alsatian. Soltner accepted, though he spoke not a word of English at the time. Moving to America, however, had a strong romantic appeal since his grandfather, who had taken part in the Great Gold Rush to Nevada and California, used to entertain his grandchildren with many a tall story of those fabled days.

Lutèce under Surmain and Soltner was an almost immediate success among the cognoscenti and the carriage trade, and it is still revered, renowned, and considered by many to be among the best restaurants in the country. André Soltner has been at Lutèce continuously since his arrival in 1961, and is the classic old-school chef/proprietor. He and his wife, Simone, live above the restaurant, and when they have friends for dinner, there they are. He is now thinking of inviting a partner chef or two to share the responsibility. "If I broke my leg skiing, what would we do?" he asks.

During his over four decades in the business he has seen many changes and styles of cuisine, and he admires creativity. "But," he says, "it took over two hundred years to develop a good base of cooking and we shouldn't forget it just for the sake of change." He is in the process of writing a book on the food of Lutèce, and it is likely that he will include the recipes he shares with us here.

Tarte Flambée
Alsatian Flammekueche

Say "*flambée*" and everyone around you will look for a great bolt of shooting flames. But *tarte flambée* is not set afire. This Alsatian savory gets its name instead from a traditional Alsatian method of baking. André Soltner says the tart used to be put into the baker's oven when it was being fired, and when the oven flared up the flames engulfed the tart and browned the top.

This recipe works perfectly well in a regular oven. You can bake *tarte flambée* as Chef André does, in four portions, or make one great big one. Either way you will have a lovely crisp bottom with a delicious creamy topping. Puff pastry is the finest pastry to use because it makes a particularly light and tender crust. With the lightly sour cheese filling and the sweet bacon/onion topping, this tart is so good you just want to eat all of it! If you don't, share it with three friends for lunch or cut it into small pieces and pass it for hors d'oeuvre.

Tarte Flambée (continued)

INGREDIENTS FOR 4
SERVINGS

For the pastry

*7 to 8 ounces puff pastry—
either store-bought or the
homemade puff pastry (see
page 121)*

For the filling

½ cup cottage cheese
½ cup crème fraîche
1 tablespoon flour
¼ teaspoon salt, or to taste
Several grindings black pepper
2 tablespoons vegetable oil

For the topping

*A 4-ounce slab of bacon, rind
removed*
Vegetable oil
*½ medium-sized onion,
quartered and sliced very
thin (about 1 cup)*

**SPECIAL EQUIPMENT
SUGGESTED**

*A food processor with steel
blade*
*A very lightly oiled pastry
sheet*

Preparing the Pastry: Lightly flour your counter, and roll the chilled dough into a 20-inch square less than ⅛-inch thick. Cut it into four disks, 8 inches across. Carefully transfer the disks to the oiled pastry sheet. Prick all over at 1-inch intervals with the tines of a table fork. Cover with plastic wrap and refrigerate for ½ hour or longer.

Preheat the oven to 425° F in time for baking.

Preparing the Filling: Drop the cottage cheese into the machine and process about ½ minute, until smooth. Add the *crème fraîche,* the flour, salt, pepper, and oil. Process again to blend, scraping down sides of the processor bowl as necessary.

Preparing the Topping: Cut the bacon into 1-inch strips and the strips into crosswise slices less than ⅛-inch thick. Oil a frying pan lightly, set over moderate heat, and stir in the bacon. Cook a minute or so, stirring and tossing, until it starts to render its fat, then stir in the onions. Toss several minutes until the onions have softened but are not yet tender—they will finish in the oven later. Let cool to tepid.

Ahead-of-Time Note: Recipe may be made a day in advance to this point. Refrigerate the filling and the bacon/onions in separate covered containers.

Assembling the Tart: Leaving a ¼-inch border free, spread the cheese mixture over the chilled pastry disks. Scatter the bacon and onions on top.

Ahead-of-Time Note: May be assembled several hours in advance. Cover loosely, and refrigerate.

Baking the Tart—15 minutes: Bake in the upper-middle level of the preheated oven for 12 to 15 minutes until the pastry is golden brown and the topping has browned lightly.

Serving Tarte Flambée: Serve hot or at room temperature.

....

COOK'S NOTES

....

....

....

....

Bacheofe
Alsatian Meat Stew

This is another example of the old-fashioned European custom of using the local baker's oven (*bacheofe*) as a second kitchen. Chef André recalls that mothers would make the dish on Sundays and let it marinate overnight. The children would then drop it off at the baker's on their way to school Monday and pick it up on their way home for lunch. During the morning, the baker put it in his oven, probably using a little of his own bread dough to seal the pot. That way the family had a hot and hearty noon meal on Mondays, even though that was always the busy day for laundry.

This *bacheofe* is traditional peasant cooking, and you may have to go to an ethnic market to find the pig's foot and tail—or omit them. You will also have to bake it in your own oven, but that's the best part because it smells so good while it's cooking.

Bacheofe (continued)

INGREDIENTS FOR 6 SERVINGS

For the meats
½ pound lamb shoulder
½ pound pork shoulder
½ pound beef chuck
If available (to give a rich texture to the sauce): a pig's foot and pig's tail, trimmed, blanched, and ready to cook

For the marinade
For the herb bouquet: 1 bay leaf, 4 sprigs fresh thyme, and 8 sprigs fresh parsley including stems
1 fairly large onion, peeled and roughly sliced
1 garlic clove, peeled, halved lengthwise, germ (central sprout) removed
¼ teaspoon salt
Freshly ground pepper
2 cups dry white wine, preferably Alsatian Riesling

For the other ingredients
1 pound all-purpose potatoes
½ pound onions
Salt and freshly ground pepper to taste
1 cup or more dry white wine
For the seal: ½ cup flour
Parsley for decoration

(continued)

Marinating the Meat: Having removed excess fat, cut the lamb, pork, and beef into 2-inch chunks. Halve the pig's foot and leave the tail as is. Make an herb bouquet by folding the bay leaf and thyme in the parsley and tying with butcher's twine. Place the meats, onion, and garlic in a roasting pan or bowl, sprinkle on the salt and pepper, and pour in the 2 cups of wine. Cover and refrigerate for 24 hours.

Assembling the Bacheofe: Preheat the oven to 300° F. Peel the potatoes and cut them into slices about ⅜-inch thick. Line the bottom of the casserole with half the potatoes. Arrange the meat over them, then the onions, and finally the rest of the potatoes. Season lightly with salt and several grinds of pepper. Discard the herb bouquet, and strain the marinade into the casserole, adding a cup or so more wine so that the liquid will come to an inch from the top of the ingredients.

Sealing the Casserole: Now, to seal the casserole hermetically and to prevent the cooking liquids from evaporating, blend the flour in a bowl with just enough water to make a soft pliable paste. Form into several rope shapes, and press them onto the rim of the casserole to seal it completely. Press the cover in place, and if the cover has a little air hole, seal that also with a piece of dough.

Baking the Bacheofe—2-½ hours: Bake in the preheated oven for 2-½ hours.

Serving the Bacheofe: Cut around under the lid to break the pastry seal—you may have to pry it open with some strength—and lift off the cover. Spoon a serving of the potatoes in the center of a hot dinner plate, then a piece of each of the meats, plus a length of the pig's tail and foot. Decorate with parsley and serve.

COOK'S NOTES

....

....

....

....

....

....

**SPECIAL EQUIPMENT
SUGGESTED**

*A covered casserole just large
     enough to hold the stew
     easily
White butcher's twine*

*Tarte Citron Mama
Lemon-Almond Tart*

There's not much to putting this dessert together if you're used to beating eggs and folding. It's easy to assemble and just very good to eat. Chef André's lemon "tarte" is made up of an almond cake bottom, a fresh lemon center, and a baked meringue top. While it's baking, the tart lemon slices seemingly melt to form a filling, and in one good bite you get the tanginess of the lemons, the sweetness of the meringue, and the subtlety of the ground almonds.

Preheat the oven to 350° F and place the rack in the lower middle level.

Preparing the Batter: Lightly butter the cake ring and baking sheet.

The Base. Beat the 3 egg yolks with the sugar until thick, pale yellow, and the mixture falls from the beater forming a slowly dissolving ribbon (this will take several minutes). Fold in the grated lemon peel, the ground almonds, and the tablespoon of flour, mixing briefly to blend.

The Egg Whites. Thoroughly wash and dry the bowl and the beaters and start beating the egg whites on moderately slow speed, adding a pinch of sugar as they foam. Increasing the speed, beat until the egg whites form stiff peaks. Stir ¼ of them into the cake base to lighten it; delicately fold in the rest.

**INGREDIENTS FOR 6
SERVINGS**

For the almond cake base
*About ½ tablespoon soft
     butter*
*3 "extra large" or 4 "large"
     eggs, separated (Chef André
     always uses "extra large")*
*¾ cup sugar (plus extra
     pinches as needed)*

(continued)

Tarte Citron Mama (continued)

The grated peel of 1 lemon
(save the lemon itself for
later)
1 cup finely ground blanched
almonds (see box)
1 tablespoon flour

For the filling
1 additional lemon

For the meringue topping
3 egg whites
¼ cup sugar
¾ cup finely ground blanched
almonds

For serving
Confectioners' sugar

**SPECIAL EQUIPMENT
SUGGESTED**

An efficient electric mixer with
a whip attachment (an
extra bowl is useful) or a
stainless steel beating bowl
and large wire whip
A 9-inch cake ring set on a
baking sheet, or a spring-
form pan

Baking the cake—20 minutes: Immediately pour the batter into the pre-pared cake ring and set in the preheated oven. Bake for 20 minutes, or until lightly browned, the top has set when you press it lightly with your finger, and the cake shows a faint line of shrinkage from the ring. It will shrink more as it cools. Leave it in the pastry ring to cool.

Ahead-of-Time Note: Tart may be prepared to this point several hours before serving.

Preparing the Filling: With a sharp paring knife, neatly cut the peel off the 2 lemons to expose the clean naked flesh. Cut the lemons into very thin crosswise slices and poke out the seeds. Arrange the slices over the top of the cake.

Preparing the Meringue Topping: (The almond cake is still in its baking ring.) Beat the egg whites until they form soft peaks. Still beating, slowly sprinkle in the ¼ cup of sugar and continue until fairly stiff peaks are formed. Gently fold in the ground almonds. Using a spatula dipped in cold water, spread the meringue over the top of the cake, being sure that it reaches to the edge of the tart all around so that the mer-ingue will not shrink during baking.

TO GRIND ALMONDS

It is easy to grind blanched almonds in an electric blender or food proces-sor, but when you attempt to grind too many at once, their natural oils begin to exude and they turn into greasy lumps. To prevent lumping, always grind them with a little of the sugar called for in your recipe. As an example, for blenders and small processors a safe amount would be ½ cup of almonds and a teaspoon of sugar, while the standard processor would take a cup of almonds and two teaspoons of sugar. Use the on-off pulse system—6 to 8 pulses should be sufficient—dump them into a bowl, and do the next batch. It goes very fast.

Baking the Meringue Topping—15 minutes: Bake the tart in the pre-heated 350° F oven for about 15 minutes, or until the meringue topping is toasty brown. Remove from the oven and let cool.

Serving Tarte Citron Mama: Serve at room temperature. Sprinkle the top with confectioners' sugar and decorate, if you wish, with a lemon-peel rose.

Jeremiah Tower

Stars, San Francisco

Jeremiah Tower has star power. His San Francisco Stars restaurant glitters; his next-door Stars Cafe sparkles; although his Stars Oakville Cafe in Napa Valley is just a glimmer at this writing, there can be little doubt that it will also join the splendid galaxy. Jeremiah's stars began to rise in the 1970s when, as chef and partner at Chez Panisse in Berkeley, he began to emphasize California and eventually regional cuisines. His concept was a natural outcome of the Chez Panisse philosophy of relying on local, seasonal ingredients, and it led to his 1986 publication of *Jeremiah Tower's New American Classics*.

As with many of today's American chefs, Jeremiah did not start out to be in a restaurant. After studying in England at King's College and then receiving a Bachelor's degree from Harvard he completed a Master of Architecture degree at Harvard Graduate School of Design. He was on his way to Hawaii to find work when a friend in San Francisco told him that Alice Waters's chef had just left and she was looking to fill the position. Although he knew nothing about the restaurant business, he loved and appreciated food, and when Alice offered him the job, he said "yes." His introduction of the "California Regional Dinner" was a rousing success and gave him and Chez Panisse a national reputation.

His skill as a restaurateur, especially since his brilliant opening of Stars on the Fourth of July, 1984, is highly acclaimed, but he's also valued as a teacher who is intent on spreading the fresh food philosophy. He has taught classes at California Culinary Academy and numerous cooking schools across the country. In 1984, he presented a week long exposition of "California Cuisine" at the Mandarin Hotel in Hong Kong. Throughout his career he has donated his talents extensively to such charity events as Meals-on-Wheels, the March of Dimes, and the Seventh on Sale for AIDS.

When we were with him, Jeremiah showed us some innovative ways with chicken.

Grilled Poussins (or Broiled Game Hens) with a Vegetable Salad and Tomato-Herb Vinaigrette

Barbecuing on the outdoor grill is certainly one of the most convivial ways to cook, and butterflied small chickens are favorite subjects. Although the recipe here speaks only of the grill, it applies just as well to the oven broiler—simply substitute "broiler" for "grill" in the following recipe. Here the birds are served with a warm salad of fresh vegetables, making it especially light and attractive in warm weather—particularly when the vegetables are young, fresh, and at their peak.

POUSSINS VS. GAME HENS

Poussins are very young and tender chickens, only about 3-½ weeks old and weighing about 1 pound. Game hens of the same weight are meatier, and one can be split in half to make two servings.

Preparing the Poussins: Using your heavy shears, cut the backbones out of the chickens and open them up. One by one, turn a bird cut side down on your work surface, and flatten it by giving it a firm pounding on the breastbone with your fist. Bend the wings akimbo, tucking the tips behind the neck. Secure the legs by cutting a 2-inch slit ½ inch from the lower end of the breast skin, then, coming through from the underside, tuck the end of each drumstick through the slit. Brush the poussin with olive oil; season with salt, pepper, and thyme leaves.

Ahead-of-Time Note: May be prepared to this point a day in advance. Arrange in a roasting pan; cover and refrigerate.

(Wash your hands and all equipment in hot soapy water before proceeding.)

Preparing the Vegetables: Using a sharp paring knife, peel the onions. Cut the cauliflower into small flowerettes, and the zucchini into quarter-inch sticks 2-½ inches long. Peel the carrots and cut into sticks the size of the zucchini. Snap the stem ends off the beans.

INGREDIENTS FOR 4
SERVINGS

For the poussins
4 poussins (or two 1-pound game hens split in half)
Olive oil, about ¼ cup
Salt and freshly ground pepper
2 teaspoons fresh thyme leaves

For the vegetable garnish
8 pearl onions
¼ head medium-sized cauliflower
2 zucchini about 8 inches long
2 medium-sized carrots
32 small green beans

(continued)

Grilled Poussins (continued)

For the vinaigrette

¼ cup (lightly pressed down)
  mixed herbs such as basil,
  marjoram, tarragon, thyme,
  fennel

¼ cup fresh lemon juice

3 tablespoons finely minced
  shallots

1 cup extra virgin olive oil

¼ teaspoon salt

¼ teaspoon freshly ground
  pepper

1 cup peeled, seeded, chopped
  tomatoes

**SPECIAL EQUIPMENT
SUGGESTED**

*A barbecue setup (or use your
  preheated oven broiler)*

Boiling the Vegetables: Chef Jeremiah likes to do each vegetable separately so that he knows each is cooked properly—just done—no crunchily half raw, undercooked vegetables for him!

While the poussin is grilling, bring 1-½ quarts of lightly salted water to the boil in a 3-quart saucepan. Drop in the pearl onions and boil slowly about 10 minutes, until just tender. Remove with a large slotted spoon, and place in a 3-quart bowl. Then drop in the cauliflower, boil for about 4 minutes, covered with a lid, until just tender; remove to the bowl and continue thus with the rest of the vegetables timing them as follows— and adding a bit more water if needed:

> zucchini, 3 minutes, uncovered
> carrots, 3 minutes, covered
> green beans, 3 or 4 minutes, uncovered

Toss together and set the bowl, uncovered, over the pan of cooking water, keeping the water at the bare simmer and tossing the vegetables gently from time to time.

Grilling (or Broiling) the Poussins: When your barbecue is ready (or your broiler hot), set the poussins flesh side facing the heat source for 5 minutes, turn, and cook another 10 minutes or until the juices from the thickest part of the thighs, when pierced, run clear.

Serving: Whisk together the vinaigrette ingredients, carefully correct seasoning, and toss with the vegetables. Arrange portions on each plate, and place a poussin on top. Chef Jeremiah suggests garlic-roasted potatoes as an accompaniment.

Poached Chicken with Mushrooms and Vegetables

Poaching means slow cooking in an aromatic broth that is at the slowest bubble. It's an ancient and lovely way to cook chicken, where the broth flavors the chicken and the chicken flavors the broth, and you get the best of both. Poaching is, in fact, the only way you can cook a mature bird, since its flesh, while full of flavor, is firm—it wants long cooking over low heat, just as though it were a cut of stewing beef. The English, by the way, call this a "boiled fowl"!

Poaching or stewing—two terms in this case for the same thing—is the easiest and most elemental of cooking methods, since you simply put the object into a pot of water and simmer until it's done. Chef Jeremiah has added some flavorful touches, such as a bacon and mushroom stuffing under the skin of the chicken, and a garnish of fresh vegetables. What a dish to diet on! And it would be entirely fat free if you left out the bacon in the stuffing—but that is really carrying things too far!

FIRST FIND YOUR HEN

Stewing hens are not always with us, and in many areas you'll have to order one unless you have chicken farms in the neighborhood. It should be under a year old—ideally around 9 months—and will weigh in at about 5 pounds.

Preparing the Chicken:

The under-skin stuffing. First mince the tarragon in the processor, then the mushrooms, and set aside in a mixing bowl. Puree half of the bacon in the machine, and cut the rest by hand into ¹⁄₁₆-inch dice. Blend tarragon, mushrooms, and bacon together, adding a little salt and pepper to taste. Loosen the chicken skin from the breast and thighs by running your fingers between them; spread the stuffing over the flesh. Truss the chicken (see box), massage the skin with soft butter, and envelop it in the washed cheesecloth.

INGREDIENTS FOR 6 SERVINGS

For the under-skin stuffing and other preparations
6 sprigs fresh tarragon (or ½ teaspoon fragrant dried tarragon)
1 pound fresh mushrooms, finely diced
½ pound raw breakfast bacon
Salt
Freshly ground pepper
5-pound stewing chicken
1 tablespoon soft butter

(continued)

Poached Chicken (continued)

For poaching the chicken
1 tablespoon salt
1 large bouquet garni
The following vegetables,
    roughly chopped:
1 medium-sized onion, peeled
2 medium-sized stalks celery
2 large peeled carrots

For the final vegetable garnish
2 medium-sized leeks
2 medium-sized turnips
4 large carrots
10 new potatoes, peeled
½ pound mushrooms

The finale
Sprigs of fresh herbs, such as
    thyme, tarragon, basil

SPECIAL EQUIPMENT
SUGGESTED

A food processor is useful
White butcher's twine
A 2-foot-square, double-
    thickness washed cheesecloth
A 3- or 4-quart kettle that
    will just hold the chicken
    easily
A 2-quart saucepan for the
    vegetables
A strainer
A warm serving platter

Poaching the Chicken—2-½ hours: Bring 2 quarts of water to the boil in the kettle with the salt, bouquet garni, and chopped vegetables. Simmer for 15 minutes, then lower in the chicken, adding a little more water if needed, to cover the chicken by half an inch. Bring again to the simmer, partially cover the kettle (it needs air circulation), and maintain the liquid at the bare simmer for 2 hours or more. Skim off scum and fat occasionally.

When Is It Done? For most of the period up to at least 2 hours, the flesh will seem very firm, then miraculously it becomes tender—the sharp prongs of a kitchen fork will pierce the fattest portion of the drumstick quite easily. Do not let it overcook.

The Vegetable Garnish: Trim the roots off the leeks; cut off and discard the green tops of the leeks down to within an inch or two of the white, or edible, portion. Cut the leeks into 1-inch crosswise pieces, being sure there is no dirt between the leaves, in which case you will have to slit and wash them. Peel the turnips, carrots, and potatoes, and cut into attractive bite-sized pieces, and halve or quarter the mushrooms. Set the vegetables aside in a bowl.

Two methods for the vegetables. Either remove the chicken when done, cover and keep warm in a 200° F oven, strain the broth into the saucepan, and cook the potatoes and vegetables in it. Or, when the chicken has cooked almost 2 hours, strain some of its stock into the saucepan, add the potatoes and simmer 5 minutes, then add the rest of the vegetables, cover the pan, and simmer 15 minutes or so, until tender.

JEREMIAH TOWER'S CHICKEN TRUSS

Provide yourself with a good 3 feet of white butcher's twine, and center it around the front end of the breast. Bring the string down the front of the shoulders, then under the armpits, and up over the shoulders again. Come down the sides of the chicken and go under the knees. Cross the string at this point and pull it tight, then wind it around the drumstick ends twice, and tie.

This is certainly one of the easiest string-trusses, and it is the perfect one for a sedentary chicken such as the bird in this recipe.

Ahead-of-Time Note: Both chicken and vegetables will stay warm in their pots for a good hour, and may be gently reheated.

Serving the Chicken: Remove the chicken from its kettle, strain and degrease the broth, and add the sprigs of fresh herbs; simmer 5 minutes. Meanwhile, unwrap the chicken and either carve and arrange the pieces on the platter in the kitchen or place the chicken on the platter and arrange the vegetables around it. Spoon some of the broth and the herbs over the chicken and vegetables, and pass the rest separately. Serve the chicken as is, or with such condiments as lemon wedges, olive oil, coarse salt, coarse mustard, capers, et cetera, or aioli (garlic mayonnaise), or Patrick Clark's tomato-cucumber mayonnaise on page 55.

COOK'S NOTES

Casserole Roasted Chicken with Garlic, Lemon, and Watercress Salad

"People who know" are often quoted as saying that the real test of a good cook is a perfectly roasted chicken. Chef Jeremiah's could well win the title, since he proposes the venerable French casserole roast, which is so perfectly suited to an ample chicken of a certain age. He oils his bird, then roasts it accompanied by garlic, lemon, and herbs in a closely covered casserole, where it steams in its own juices, while garlic, herbs, and lemon all fuse together with chicken. At the end he uncovers the casserole to brown the chicken and let its heavenly aromas fill the room.

INGREDIENTS FOR 6 SERVINGS

For the chicken

A 5-½- to 6-pound roaster chicken

Salt and freshly ground pepper

½ cup olive oil

5 large heads of garlic, separated into cloves, unpeeled

3 sprigs fresh rosemary

4 lemons, halved crosswise

For the salad

¼ cup very fresh-tasting walnut oil

Salt

Freshly ground pepper

12 bunches watercress

(continued)

TIMING: Count on a good 2 hours in all—1 hour for covered roasting, ½ hour for browning, and a 30-minute rest before carving.

Preparing the Chicken: Preheat the oven to 375° F. Place all ingredients and equipment beside your main work area on a large tray or newspapers, and plan to dispose of and/or wash everything (including your hands) thoroughly with soap and hot water when you are through.

Remove the packet of giblets in the cavity, and reserve for something else. Remove any visible clumps of fat from inside the cavity, wash and dry them in paper towels, and set aside. Wash the chicken both inside and out under cold running water; dry thoroughly with paper towels.

Salt and pepper the cavity lightly, pour in a spoonful of olive oil and stuff in a handful of garlic and rosemary. Squeeze in the juice of a lemon, and add the lemon halves. Truss the chicken—Chef Jeremiah's easy string truss is described in the box on page 40. Brush the chicken with olive oil, sprinkle with salt and pepper, and set it breast up in the casserole. Flatten the reserved pieces of chicken fat with your fist and lay them over the breast. Smash the rest of the garlic cloves with the flat of your big knife and lay them also over the chicken along with the remaining rosemary. Squeeze on the rest of the lemons, tossing the squeezed halves into the casserole.

Ahead-of-Time Note: The chicken is now ready for the oven, and may be prepared to this point two hours ahead.

Roasting the Chicken—1-½ hours: Set the covered casserole in the lower third of the preheated oven. Basting is really not necessary, but a quick peak now and then is useful just to see how things are going. You may also wish a quick basting with the accumulated juices, using a bulb baster.

After an hour, remove the cover and turn the thermostat up to 400° F. Continue roasting and letting the chicken brown.

When Is It Done? The thighs will be fairly tender when pressed; the drumsticks will move up and down in their sockets fairly well. When the bird is lifted, the last juices to fall from the vent end will be clear yellow with no trace of rose.

Remove the chicken to the serving platter, cut off the trussing strings, and return the chicken to the turned-off oven, leaving the door ajar.

Preparing the Sauce and Serving the Roasted Chicken and Salad: Drain the juices from the casserole through a sieve. Using a ladle, push the garlic to extract juice from it as well. Skim the fat off the surface in the remaining juices of the strained liquid. Whisk in the walnut oil and season to taste with salt and pepper. Toss the watercress into the sauce to coat well. Place the seasoned watercress around the chicken and drizzle with any remaining sauce. Serve immediately.

Note: Garlic-roasted potatoes would be an appropriate accompaniment.

SPECIAL EQUIPMENT
SUGGESTED

A covered casserole or roaster just large enough to hold the chicken comfortably
A bulb baster
A pastry brush
An oven-proof serving platter

Lidia Bastianich

Felidia, New York

"I was raised in a world where food was the center of life, where everyone's labor and activity centered on the feeding of the family." Her world was Istria, the Adriatic peninsula that was part of Italy before being annexed by Yugoslavia in 1946. There she learned to prepare regional dishes from her grandmother and her mother. Later, her great-aunt, Nina, the cook for a wealthy family, taught Lidia refinements.

Frustrated by the geopolitical conditions of living in an annexed country, Lidia's family left, and by the time they were accepted for relocation to the United States, Lidia, at age eleven, had a year's experience in a professional kitchen. Lidia still remembers seeing her first New York City Horn & Hardart Automat where the food sat in little glass cubbies that opened with the deposit of a coin. "I loved it. To a little kid from Istria, it was magic."

By the time she met and married Felice, also from Istria, Lidia was so well versed in the workings of a restaurant that the young couple felt ready to launch one of their own. They operated two popular restaurants in Queens before opening Felidia in Manhattan.

Lidia is a natural teacher and has taken and taught college courses in food anthropology and physiology. As this warm and knowledgeable chef moves through the preparation of a recipe, bits of history, information on techniques, and instructions for choosing the best products flow naturally. She carefully inspects pasta for its sheen, adeptly pours a drop of olive oil into her palms, rubs them together, and wafts them in front of her face to test the aroma. This is a chef who cares deeply about her profession. The results are the dishes she gives us here—the *orecchiette* (little ears pasta) with bitter greens and sweet sausage, and the creamy risotto, intense with the flavor of woodsy mushrooms, as well as the opening recipe (not shown on TV) of Istrian seafood pasta tasting of the ocean.

Capellini all'Istriana
Angel-Hair Pasta with
Seafood Sauce

Capellini all'Istriana is a perfect illustration of how delicious pasta can be with just a few simple but carefully chosen ingredients. This light, well-balanced dish, named for Lidia Bastianich's seaside hometown in Italy, doesn't have too much of anything but everything it does have is carefully selected. The seafood is impeccably fresh, the tomatoes taste like tomatoes, and the angel-hair spaghetti has no blotchy, dull, or broken pieces.

Keep the shellfish iced down until you are ready to cook, and for the freshest flavor don't cook it until you are ready to eat it. The tomatoes, of course, could be fixed ahead, but the whole dish is so fast to prepare that you might as well do it all at once and save the time for something else.

Preparing the Seafood:

The Shrimp. Shell the shrimp. If a black vein runs along the curve of the back, slit down the back and remove it.

The Scallops. Cut off and discard the hard little white nubbin attached to the side of the scallops, and slice the scallops in half horizontally.

The Clams. For easier opening, set the clams in the freezer for 20 minutes to relax the muscle that clamps the shells together. Holding the clam over a bowl to catch its juices, set it in the palm of your left hand, the hinge end with its indentation toward you. Hold the clam knife in your right hand, its blade poised between the shells at the opposite end, and guided by the fingers of your left hand. With the clam secure in your left hand, force the blade between the shells, then cut around under the top shell to release the muscle. Rotate the blade between the shells to force them open. Run the blade under the body of clam to release and remove it. Pour juices into a bowl, chop the clams, place in a separate bowl, and reserve.

Preparing the Tomato Sauce:

The Garlic. Peel and crush the garlic—Chef Lidia lays the clove on her work surface and presses hard on it with the heel of one hand with additional pressure from the palm of the other.

INGREDIENTS FOR 6 SERVINGS

For the shellfish

1 pound medium-sized headless shrimp

½ pound sea scallops

15 littleneck clams

For the sauce

6 large garlic cloves

2 cups crushed peeled tomatoes (fresh Italian plum tomatoes plus whole peeled canned tomatoes)

6 tablespoons good olive oil

1 teaspoon crushed hot red pepper flakes

3 to 4 tablespoons chopped Italian parsley

(continued)

Angel Hair Pasta (continued)

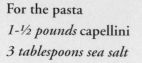

For the pasta
1-½ pounds capellini
3 tablespoons sea salt

**SPECIAL EQUIPMENT
SUGGESTED**

*2 heavy 12-inch frying pans
A tall stockpot of at least 2-
     gallon capacity
A warm serving bowl, or
     individual plates*

The Tomatoes. If your tomatoes are fully ripe, the flavor of your sauce should need no help from the can. However, if it's to be mostly canned the inclusion of even a few imperfect fresh plum tomatoes gives the sauce an illusion of freshness—that fateful decision is yours to make. In any case, fresh tomatoes should be peeled, quartered lengthwise, then seeded; canned plum tomatoes also need seeding.

Simmering the Sauce. Set one of the frying pans over moderate heat. Add 2 tablespoons olive oil and brown the crushed garlic very lightly. Add the tomatoes and pepper flakes, and let simmer for 20 minutes.

Preparing the Seafood Sauce: Pour 2 tablespoons of olive oil into the second frying pan and set over moderately high heat. Stir in the shrimp and scallops, and sauté 30 seconds to evaporate excess moisture, then stir in the clams and almost immediately pour in the clam juice, being careful not to include any sand at the bottom of the container. Raise heat to high and shake the pan, until the liquid comes to the boil. Correct seasoning. Pour in the tomato sauce, bring again to the boil, shaking the pan. Check seasoning again, then pour on 2 tablespoons of fresh olive oil and stir in parsley. Set aside.

Ahead-of-Time Note: May be completed ½ hour in advance to this point—it loses its fresh taste when it sits around much longer.

Boiling the Pasta—3 minutes: Heat 6 quarts of water in the stockpot, adding the salt, and timing so that the water is at the full boil by the time the shellfish is ready in the previous step. Then stir the *capellini* into the boiling water—it takes only 2 to 3 minutes to cook.

Serving Capellini all'Istriana: Drain the cooked pasta and toss immediately with the hot sauce.

DRIED PASTA

Buying Pasta

Lots of people like to claim that they only buy fresh pasta, but Italians know that fresh and dry are equally good and they use them both. Dried pasta, *pasta secca*, is made from 100 percent durum wheat semolina, water, and salt. The secret of good commercial dry pasta is in the working and the drying, and the best will have a golden color and a lively, almost translucent sheen. Look for a package or box with no pieces that are broken, chipped, blotchy, or dull.

Cooking Pasta

Do not add oil to pasta while it is cooking and do not rinse after it is cooked because the starch that clings to the pasta will bind it to the sauce. A pound of pasta should be cooked in a tall pot in 5 to 6 quarts of rapidly boiling salted water. (Chef Lidia uses 1 tablespoon of salt for every 2 quarts of water, but you should taste the water to determine its saltiness.) Once the pasta is stirred into the water, cover the pot so the water will return quickly to the boil, then set the cover ajar to finish cooking. (Chef Lidia places a wooden spoon between the lid and the pot.) The pasta should be cooked according to *your* taste; eat several pieces to be sure and when done drain at once and proceed with the recipe. (Since it will be tossed with the sauce in a pan over heat to equalize the temperatures, drain it when it is just slightly short of being fully cooked.)

Orecchiette con Broccoli di Rape e Salsicce
Pasta Ears with Broccoli di Rape and Sausages

This lovely dish shows what can happen to tough old greens if you treat them right. When *broccoli di rape* is prepared the way Chef Lidia prepares it—peeled and cooked long enough—it has an agreeable slight bitterness that blends wonderfully with the sweetness of the sausage and the full ripeness of the cheese.

It is important to match the shapes of pasta to the sauce. Thin sauces are best with flat pastas; other shapes have nooks and crannies to catch pieces of chunkier sauces. *Orecchiette*, which means "little ears," are just right to pick up all the tasty bits of sauce in this dish.

Pasta Ears (continued)

INGREDIENTS FOR 6
SERVINGS

For the sauce

2 pounds broccoli di rape

½ pound sweet Italian sausage

5 tablespoons good olive oil

3 large garlic cloves, crushed

Salt

*¼ teaspoon hot red pepper
flakes*

*1 to 3 tablespoons unsalted
butter (optional)*

*1 cup or more excellent
chicken stock*

For the pasta

6 quarts water

3 tablespoons salt

1 pound orecchiette pasta

For serving

*1 ounce or more pecorino
Romano cheese, grated just
before using, and you may
want to pass around more
separately*

SPECIAL EQUIPMENT
SUGGESTED

*A 12-inch sauté pan, 3 inches
deep, with tight-fitting
cover*

*A tall stockpot holding at least
2 gallons, with cover*

*A large warm platter, or warm
soup bowls or plates*

Preparing the Broccoli di Rape: Wash and spin-dry the broccoli di rape and remove the large tough leaves, leaving just tender leaves and flower buds. Cut off and discard the lower part of the stems, leaving the broccoli about 8 inches long. Peel the stems by lifting strips from the stem end and drawing them up toward the bud area—a perfect peel is not necessary, but removing peel does remove bitterness.

Preparing the Sauce: Peel the sausage, crumble it, and sauté over moderately high heat in a tablespoon of olive oil. In a moment or two, add the crushed garlic and continue sautéing for another 2 to 3 minutes, until the sausage is lightly browned. Drain out the fat in the pan, and add the remaining olive oil. Roughly line up the broccoli di rape and slice into 4-inch lengths; add to the pan, tossing. Taste, and season lightly with salt and pepper flakes. (At this point, you could start the pasta.) Cover the broccoli pan and let steam for several minutes; when the broccoli has wilted, stir in the butter, then the stock, and bring to the boil. Taste again for seasoning, and let cook uncovered for several minutes more to reduce and concentrate the liquid. Again taste and correct seasoning. Set aside until the pasta is ready.

Boiling the Pasta: Heat 6 quarts of water in the stockpot, adding the salt, and timing so that the water is at the full boil by the time the broccoli di rape goes into the pan in the previous step. With the heat at its maximum, stir in the pasta and cover the pan until the water is at the boil. Then set the cover ajar and maintain at a moderate boil for 10 to 12

HARD GRATING CHEESE

Parmesan, *parmigiano*, and Romano, *pecorino Romano*, are the best known of the hard grating cheeses and the ones most often used in Italian cooking. Parmesan is made from cow's milk and Romano from sheep's milk. Sheep's milk cheeses have an intense flavor and are best used for dishes with a sharp flavor, such as Chef Lidia's *orecchiette* with broccoli rape in which the bitter greens need the sharpness of the Romano.

Grating cheeses lose their freshness very quickly when they are exposed to air, and Chef Lidia grates them as needed by hand on the medium side of a freestanding cheese grater. If you absolutely have to grate cheese ahead, immediately wrap it in a tightly closed plastic bag and freeze it for as short a time as possible.

Grated cheese should not be added to the pasta when it is heating in the pan with the sauce since it can stick to the pan and leave an unpleasant taste. Instead, grate it on the pasta when it is in the serving dish and put a good big chunk with a grater on the table.

minutes, stirring and checking on the progress now and then. After 9 minutes, start testing by eating a piece. It should just be cooked through, but not quite as tender as you would like because it will cook a little more with the sauce to come. Drain at once, and proceed to the serving.

Serving the Pasta: Reheat the broccoli di rape as soon as the pasta has cooked and drained. Turn the hot pasta into the hot sauce and toss gently to blend. Taste carefully for seasoning, and remove from heat.

Sprinkle on half the freshly grated Romano cheese, and toss to blend.

At once, turn the pasta onto the hot platter, bowls or plates, sprinkle with the rest of the Romano, and serve.

Risotto ai Funghi Selvatici
Risotto with Wild Mushrooms

This is a sumptuous dish—a risotto to dream about. It has a deep, rich mushroom taste and a magnificent creamy texture. This is what risotto is all about.

Although it is more often seen as a first course, risotto makes a splendid main course. People seem to avoid serving it this way because they don't want to deal with the time and frustrations of last-minute cooking. A real risotto requires your almost full attention while it is cooking and loses its unique creaminess if it sits around and the rice becomes flabby as the grains absorb more liquid. The Italians say, "Don't let the risotto wait for you at the doorstep," meaning that you are to be at the table when the cooking is finished. The solution, of course, is to invite everyone into the kitchen to sip a glass of wine while the risotto bubbles.

Risotto (continued)

INGREDIENTS FOR 6
SERVINGS

For the mushrooms
¼ cup dry porcini mushrooms
½ cup strong hot chicken stock
12 ounces wild mushrooms
    (porcini, shiitakes,
    chanterelles, et cetera)
2 tablespoons olive oil
½ teaspoon salt

For the rice
3 tablespoons olive oil
1 cup minced onions
2 tablespoons minced shallots
2 cups Arborio rice
1 cup dry white wine
About 6 cups strong hot
    chicken stock
Salt

For serving
2 to 4 tablespoons butter, cut
    into pieces
1 cup freshly grated, best-
    quality Parmesan cheese
Freshly ground pepper

Preparing the Mushrooms: Rinse the dry porcini mushrooms, then soak in a bowl with ½ cup hot chicken stock and set aside for 20 minutes. Trim the fresh wild mushrooms, discarding tough woody areas and damaged portions. (If necessary, wash briefly, and dry in a towel.) Cut them into ⅛-inch, lengthwise slices. Film the frying pan with olive oil. When hot, toss in the wild mushrooms, season with salt, and sauté 5 minutes or more to evaporate moisture and to intensify their flavor.

Preparing the Risotto—15 to 20 minutes from the time the rice goes in: Meanwhile, heat 3 tablespoons of oil in the sauté pan and add the onions. Sauté, stirring frequently, until translucent, then add the shallots and sauté for a moment more. Finally, stir in the rice, and "toast it" by stirring rather slowly and fairly constantly over moderately high heat until the grains begin to turn golden, and to feel loose and dry—they will click softly in the pan. At once, add the wine; turn the heat fairly high to boil it down. When the rice is almost dry, ladle in enough hot stock barely to cover it. Regulate heat so that the stock just simmers, season with a little salt, and prepare to be near it and to stir it slowly and almost constantly from now on.

Adding the Mushrooms: Continue to add stock as the rice absorbs it, and after the rice has cooked for about 8 minutes, stir in the sautéed wild mushrooms. Ladle ½ cup of stock into the sauté pan to deglaze it, and pour the liquid into the risotto. Remove the soaked porcini and squeeze their juices back into their bowl. Chop the porcini and stir into the risotto; then, being careful not to add any sand or sediment at the bottom of the bowl, pour the soaking juices into the risotto.

When Is It Done? The rice grains will have doubled in size and are suspended in a creamy liquid, colored by the mushrooms—a carefully cooked risotto looks like nothing else. Taste the rice: it should be just tender with the slightest texture or resistance as you bite through a grain—what the Italians call "*al dente*" or "to the tooth"—but should be creamy.

Serving the Risotto: Remove from heat, and immediately beat in the butter and half the cheese with a wooden spoon. Season with pepper to taste, serve immediately on a warm platter or warm soup plates, and sprinkle with Parmesan—pass the rest separately.

Words of Wisdom: You may have to do it 2 or 3 times to get the feel of how long to cook it and how creamy it should be. Remembering that this is a dish that stands by itself—not an accompaniment—it must have a fine strong flavor.

SPECIAL EQUIPMENT SUGGESTED

A 2-quart saucepan for hot chicken stock

A small ladle

A 10-inch frying pan

A heavy 12- by 4-inch sauté pan or casserole

A flat-ended wooden spoon or spatula for stirring the rice

A warm serving bowl or wide soup plates

RISOTTO

Chef Lidia has really taken the mystery out of making perfect risotto every time.

The Pot: The pot must be heavy on the bottom, not too deep, and about 12 inches wide to allow for evaporation. Sides 4 to 5 inches high will keep the heat in the pot even.

The Rice: Short grain, starchy rice, such as the Italian *Arborio*, is necessary in order to make a creamy risotto. A fat opaque center—*la perla*—indicates a good starch content.

The Liquid: Wine is always the first liquid to be added, because all of the first liquid will be absorbed by the rice and the high acidity balances the starch and adds to the good flavor of the risotto. The stock should complement the filling—fish stock for seafood or light chicken for vegetables, for example. The stock should be hot and 3 times the amount of rice.

The Method: The rice is always "toasted" first to seal the starch, so that it will release slowly—Chef Lidia refers to this as creating a "time capsule." The liquid is added slowly, so that the starch will release gradually to create creaminess. It does not work if you add all the liquid at once.

The Finish: Risotto can be very loose, or, as the Italians say, "*all'onda*," like the waves in the sea, or it can be a little drier. Usually risottos with fillings from the sea are served *all'onda* while those with inland fillings, such as wild mushrooms, are served somewhat denser—but still creamy.

Patrick Clark

The Hay-Adams, Washington, D.C.

Patrick Clark's father, an accomplished New York chef who had worked for a number of fine New York restaurants, tried to discourage his son from a like career. But Patrick was determined. "It was never considered a glamourous profession," he remembers. "Not until 'executive chef' was reclassified as a white-collar job and chefs began to be celebratized, did it become more desirable."

His training started at New York City's Technical College, where the director recognized Patrick's talents and encouraged him to study abroad. "When you begin you're not really sure of your own talents until somebody takes you under his wing and says you've got the hands or the right attitude for this."

Young Patrick followed the advice about going abroad, and found an apprenticeship in England, but it was in France, with renowned chef Michel Guérard at Eugénie les Bains, that he found the inspiration that sparked his career. Patrick says, "That was a total revelation for me. What really impressed me was the care and intensity with which food was handled. It was a mind-blowing experience."

After his return to this country he began an impressive succession of journeyman positions at Régine's, Le Coup de Fusil, La Boîte, and the Pear Tree. "When you work with somebody for a while you're inspired, so almost eighty percent of your food mirrors that person's until you find your own style." His own style—contemporary American based on solid French technique and influences "from anywhere that good food is produced"—came of age when he opened the popular bistros Odéon and Café Luxembourg in New York. "That really made me."

Although there have been black chefs cooking in restaurant kitchens for years, few have chosen to follow the path of formal education and European apprenticeships as Patrick did. To foster those opportunities, Patrick is deeply involved with the United Culinary Federation in their efforts to raise money to establish culinary scholarships for Afro-Americans.

Now executive chef at the Hay-Adams in Washington, D.C., Chef Patrick Clark has definitely established himself as one of the leaders in his profession, and we are fortunate here to have his imaginative Salmon Roulade, and his crusty way with the usually mild grouper.

Seared Peppered Salmon Roulade with Gazpacho Sauce

Patrick Clark's charming roulades of salmon fillet with their flecks of cracked black pepper, curls of white leeks tucked inside, and festive red and green vegetables make it an outstanding and attractive appetizer or luncheon dish. The Japanese sushi technique inspired the idea for the salmon and Spanish gazpacho was Clark's motivation for the sauce. Wrapping the salmon in foil before pan-searing keeps its shape, a method that he learned as a Boy Scout cooking over an open fire.

Chef Patrick likes to use Norwegian farm-raised salmon for this recipe because he can rely on the consistency of their size and quality. He has prepared the same recipe with fresh tuna, and has also done it by rolling a very thin slice of tuna inside the salmon.

Preparing the Leek Filling: Julienne the white of the leeks (see following recipe, page 58), then sauté slowly in the butter, until limp and tender.

Preparing the Salmon:

Trimming the Salmon. Set the salmon on a sheet of parchment paper. Remove any little bones from the thick top part of the salmon by rubbing your finger searchingly over the surface to locate them and pulling them out with your pliers. You now want to butterfly the fish. Starting at one of the long sides, make a horizontal cut with a sharp knife, and continue to cut within an inch of the opposite side—keep top and bottom layers as even in thickness as you can.

INGREDIENTS FOR 6 SERVINGS

For the leek filling
2 leeks, 1 inch in diameter
1 tablespoon butter

For the salmon
A 3-pound center-cut fine fresh salmon fillet trimmed to a perfect rectangle

(continued)

Salmon Roulade (continued)

Kosher salt

¼ cup of cracked black pepper

2 tablespoons olive oil

2 tablespoons or more
  peanut oil

For the sauce

10 to 12 ripe red plum
  tomatoes

1 large cucumber, unwaxed

2 cups mayonnaise (preferably
  homemade with olive oil)

¼ cup or so chilled mineral
  water

2 teaspoons of lemon juice

⅛ teaspoon of Cayenne pepper

Salt

Freshly ground white pepper

A few drops of red wine
  vinegar

For the garnish

1 red pepper

1 cucumber

2 or 3 ripe plum tomatoes

8 to 10 chives, finely minced

Salt

Freshly ground pepper

Pounding the Salmon: Open the salmon like a book and cover its surface with a piece of plastic wrap. Pound evenly but firmly all over the surface to a thickness of about ½ inch. Remove plastic wrap and sprinkle 1-½ teaspoons of Kosher salt over the surface and only a small pinch of the pepper. Scatter on the leeks evenly, to make a sparse covering.

Forming the Roulade: Using the parchment paper under the salmon to help you, roll the salmon up on itself to make a very tight cylinder. Then roll it up again tightly in the parchment, twist the paper at the two ends, and tie the ends with the twine. To firm up the roulade, refrigerate for at least 1 hour (preferably, 2 hours).

Ahead-of-Time Note: May be done in advance to this point but only up to a day ahead—refrigerate in a plastic bag.

The Pepper Coating: Spread the sheet of aluminum foil on your work area and paint the entire surface of the foil with a light coating of olive oil. When the roulade is well chilled, cut off the ends of the parchment with scissors and unwrap the fish onto the foil. Sprinkle with the cracked pepper, pressing it all over the surface. Now wrap very tightly in the foil, twisting the ends tightly. Refrigerate until cooking time.

Preparing the Sauce:

Fresh Tomato and Fresh Cucumber Juice. For tomato juice, wash the tomatoes and cut in half lengthwise. Drop them into the food processor and process a minute or more, until completely pureed. Pour into the sieve, and push hard with a ladle or spoon to extract all possible juice out of the remains. Do the same with the unpeeled cucumber—its green skin will give a nice color.

Mixing the Sauce: Whisking the mayonnaise in a 3-quart bowl, pour in the tomato and then the cucumber juices, adding a little of the mineral water to make a loose creamy sauce that will only be thick enough to coat the back of a spoon. Whisk in the rest of the sauce ingredients and correct seasoning. Cover and chill several hours, so that its flavors will blend. Taste, and correct seasoning again before serving.

Ahead-of-Time Note: May be made 2 or 3 days in advance; after that, the vegetable juices will begin to go off in flavor.

Preparing the Garnish:

The Red Pepper. Set the red pepper in a baking dish under a hot broiler, turning as it blisters and blackens on all sides. Remove from the oven, seal the dish with plastic wrap and let steam 10 minutes, then scrape off the skin. Remove core and seeds, cut into lengthwise ¼-inch strips, then cut the strips into dice.

The Cucumber. Peel the cucumber, and halve lengthwise; scrape out and discard the seeds. Cut into ¼-inch strips, then the strips into dice. Drop into a saucepan of boiling water, bring rapidly to the boil again, drain immediately, and refresh in cold water. Drain thoroughly.

The Plum Tomatoes. Peel, seed, and dice the tomatoes.

Toss the diced pepper, cucumbers, and tomatoes together in a bowl eith the chopped chives and a sprinkling of salt and pepper.

SPECIAL EQUIPMENT SUGGESTED

Parchment paper
Small needle-nosed pliers, for bone removal
Plastic wrap
A meat pounder, or heavy flat-bottomed pan
White butcher's twine
A sheet of aluminum foil, 12 inches by about 24 inches
Food processor
A fine-meshed sieve
A 12-inch, no-stick sauté pan
Large metal tongs for turning salmon
A long sharp knife

PURCHASING FRESH FISH FILLETS

Selecting and storing fish fillets is something every serious cook should know how to do.

If your trip to the market means that you will be out for a while, take a plastic container with ice and a couple of plastic bags along with you. Inspect the fish carefully. Whether the fillets are sitting naked or in Styrofoam packages, they should be on ice and not in a pool of water or piled high on top of other fish. They should smell like fresh sea breeze, not "fishy" or astringent, and be translucent without dark spots or bruises. Feel them. Fresh fish fillets have a moist, elastic touch, not a mushy or mealy one: they will hold an impression from your finger.

When you have selected your perfectly fresh fish fillets, place them in one of your plastic bags, seal it tightly, and lay it in the container on top of the ice. Fill the second bag with more ice and lay that on top of the fish. This is exactly how you should store the fish in your refrigerator or in the back of your car if you are out for a while.

Since you don't know what fish will be fresh when you get to the market, you should know what species are good substitutes for each other. Chef Patrick uses the mild-flavored grouper for one of his recipes. Good substitutes are snapper, halibut, or sole. Thin slices of tuna or swordfish will pound out nicely in place of the salmon in fish roulade.

Salmon Roulade (continued)

Cooking the Salmon—4 minutes: Set the sauté pan over moderately high heat, add the peanut oil, and when hot lay the salmon roll in it. Turn the roll almost continuously in the pan for 3 to 4 minutes, or until when you press it the contents have changed from squashy raw to slightly resistant. Remove from the pan—the heat retained by the foil will take the salmon to medium rare. Let cool to room temperature, about 1 hour.

Serving: Taste the sauce and give your final approval—it probably needs a little more salt. Leaving on its foil covering, cut off the end piece of the salmon roll (this piece will not be served). With your long sharp knife, make crosswise slices ¾-inch thick, cutting right through the foil. As you plate them, unroll and remove the foil covering from the salmon slices. Arrange 2 on each plate, ladle a generous amount of sauce around the salmon, and sprinkle a handful of the colorful garnish over the sauce.

Horseradish-Crusted Grouper with Old-fashioned Mashed Potatoes, Chive Oil, and Crisp-Fried Julienne of Leeks

Patrick Clark's grouper with horseradish crust became his signature dish when he was chef at Bice in Los Angeles. It's the kind of creation he finds challenging—transforming a mild-flavored fish such as grouper into something pungent and interesting to eat. Chef Patrick coats one side of the fish in bread crumbs seasoned with freshly grated horseradish and he uses a chive oil sauce as a flavor booster. The horseradish and chives give the fish a piquancy that the chef then tames with a buttery bed of mashed potatoes. A crowning nest of crisp-fried julienne of leeks is a dramatic finish to this balance of tastes and textures.

Preliminaries:

Preparing the Chive Oil. Puree the chives and oil in the electric blender, until very smooth. Refrigerate in a squeeze bottle or covered jar, where it will keep for about 2 weeks.

The Crust. Remove the peel from a portion of the horseradish and rub the peeled area through the coarse side of a grater. Turn ¾ cup of the grated horseradish into one of the flat dishes with the crumbs and mix in the herbs. Whisk the milk and eggs together and pour into a second dish. Spread the seasoned flour in the last dish.

Coating the Fish. It is the top side of the fish that gets the coating because the top has a more attractive shape; this is the side where the bone—not the skin—was. Season this side of each fillet with salt and pepper. Dredge this top side only in the flour, shaking off the excess; coat the same side with the eggs and milk, and finally drop into the crumb mixture, pressing firmly to make sure it adheres. Set on a tray, cover with plastic wrap, and refrigerate until cooking time.

INGREDIENTS FOR 6 SERVINGS

For the chive oil
20 chives cut into 2-inch pieces
1 cup canola oil

For the grouper and crust
A 4- to 5-inch piece of fresh
   horseradish
2-½ cups crumbs from dry
   French bread (crust
   included)
1 tablespoon chopped parsley
1 tablespoon chopped fresh
   rosemary
1 tablespoon chopped fresh
   thyme
½ cup milk
2 eggs

(continued)

Horseradish-Crusted Grouper (continued)

Seasoned flour (2 cups flour,
    1-½ teaspoons salt,
    ¾ teaspoon freshly ground
    pepper)
6 grouper fillets, 7 ounces each
    (or halibut, sole, or red
    snapper)
Salt
Freshly ground black pepper
Canola oil, for cooking

For the crisp julienne of leeks
4 medium-sized leeks (1-inch
    circumference)
Fine fresh peanut oil

For the mashed potatoes
1 tablespoon Kosher salt, plus
    more for seasoning the
    potatoes
2-½ pounds Yukon Gold
    potatoes (or baking
    potatoes), peeled and
    quartered
Freshly ground black pepper
1 stick (4 ounces) unsalted
    butter, diced
2 cups hot milk, more if
    necessary

(continued)

Preparing the Crisp Julienne of Leeks Garnish: Cut the root end off the leeks, and cut the white part into 3-½-inch lengths. Halve lengthwise, and cut into fine julienne. Drop into cold water, leave a moment, lift out with your hands (leaving any sand behind), and gently squeeze out excess water; fluff up. Heat 2 inches of peanut oil to 325° F in the frying pan and drop in the leeks. Let them cook slowly, until the bubbling stops, about 5 minutes. Remove with a skimmer and drain on paper towel. The leeks do not brown; they remain light and crisp, with a hint of sweetness.

The Mashed Potatoes: Preheat the oven to 300° F. Bring 4 quarts of water to the boil in the kettle and add a tablespoon of Kosher salt. Add the potatoes and boil slowly for about 20 minutes, until just tender. Drain the potatoes thoroughly, place on the baking pan, and set uncovered in the oven to dry out, shaking and tossing several times. Remove the potatoes from the oven and puree through the vegetable mill into a large saucepan (Chef Patrick prefers the vegetable mill to the potato ricer). Season with salt and pepper, then begin beating in pieces of butter with a wooden spoon, alternating with little additions of hot milk. Check seasoning, and keep warm in a double boiler with cover ajar—it needs air circulation.

Cooking the Fish—About 7 minutes: Heat ½ inch of canola oil to medium high in the large no-stick pan. Place the fish fillets crust side down in the hot oil, and cook rather slowly, until golden brown, about 3 minutes. Turn and continue to cook 3 to 4 minutes longer on the other side.

When Is It Done? When it has begun to feel springy to the touch in contrast to its squashy raw state. If you have doubts, cut into a piece—the flesh should be opaque throughout rather than translucent.

Remove the fish and drain on paper towels.

HERBED OILS

Patrick Clark's herbed oils are quick and easy flavor boosters for fish, meat, or poultry. Make them in advance and store covered in the refrigerator for up to two weeks. Chef Patrick stores his in plastic squeeze bottles, which makes it fast and fun to squirt the oil on whatever dish you want to enhance.

Flavor the oil according to your taste and blend several together or store them separately. You can squeeze a variety of them on a finished dish. Cover the refrigerated oils tightly, so they won't pick up flavors or aromas from the refrigerator. Shake them to reemulsify before using. Herbs to try include basil, mint, oregano, sage, or tarragon, as well as the chives.

Serving: Spoon a serving of mashed potatoes directly into the center of each plate. Place the fish, crust side up, on top. Drizzle chive oil around the mashed potatoes and top the fish with a nest of leeks. Serve immediately.

SPECIAL EQUIPMENT
SUGGESTED

An electric blender

A squeeze bottle or a covered jar

A freestanding 4-sided grater

3 flat dishes, such as oval baking dishes or large pie plates

A 12- by 3-inch pan for frying leeks

A 6-quart kettle

A 9- by 13-inch baking pan

A vegetable mill

A 12-inch, no-stick sauté pan

Michel Richard

Citrus, Los Angeles

Michel Richard and his wife, Laurence, making cookies with their children at home.

When Michel Richard enters his house he likes to have it smell of cooking. It makes him happy. This may seem odd for a man who spends so much of his time running his flagship restaurant, Citrus in Los Angeles, and its offspring in Santa Barbara, Washington, D.C., and Baltimore —all called Citronelle. His energy and enthusiasm as chef, pâtissier, and restaurant owner are infectious and when he walks into one of his kitchens or restaurants it is obvious that everyone adores him, and he, in turn, treats his staff like family and his guests like his very special friends.

Michel Richard can't imagine being anything but a chef, and he's known it since he was seven. He began his culinary apprenticeship in his native France when he was thirteen in a pastry shop that was part of a restaurant, and at the end of six years he had completed training not just in the art of pastry making but in all aspects of the restaurant business. It was his love and natural talent for baking that led him to Paris and to the renowned establishment of master pâtissier Gaston Lenôtre. Lenôtre so much appreciated young Michel that he sent him off to manage the newly opened Lenôtre pastry shop in New York, and Michel has lived in the United States ever since.

Next he moved to Santa Fe, New Mexico, and opened the "French Pastry Shop" in the La Fonda hotel. Moving ever westward, he then left a booming business for Los Angeles and opened yet another successful pastry shop, where he became an almost instant success.

To have experienced such success in both his restaurants and his pastry shops it might seem that Chef Michel has a secret source of rare and unusual ingredients. Quite the contrary. He simply uses—and prides himself on using—the very best he can find. No butter substitutes, ersatz cream, and fake chocolate for him, as you will see when you try his Chocolate Dome and Hot Chocolate Truffles that follow.

The Chocolate Dome

Hiding under Michel Richard's beautiful chocolate dome is an orange-soaked sponge cake layered with a soft chocolate mousse. With its smooth surface and handsome leaf and raspberry decorations, it is a splendid dessert that looks very professional indeed, but as you will see, is not that difficult to produce. This is a great teaching recipe, too, since it deals with many aspects of chocolate, from melting to fillings and coating to the hows of real chocolate leaves.

Preparing the Génoise Sponge Cake: Preliminaries. Using the pastry brush, butter the bowl quite generously. Sprinkle in several tablespoons of flour and rotate the bowl in all directions to coat the entire inner surface, then turn the bowl upside down and knock out excess flour. Preheat the oven to 350° F.

The Cake Batter: Beat the eggs and sugar in the bowl of the mixer for 5 minutes, until thick, fluffy, and tripled in volume. (Information on beating whole eggs and sugar is on page 134.) Rapidly sift and fold in the flour with a big rubber spatula, and scoop the batter into the prepared bowl.

Baking the Cake: Bake in the middle level of the preheated 350° F oven for 35 to 45 minutes.

When Is It Done? When a toothpick, stuck through the center of the cake, comes out clean. Turn the cake out on a rack to cool completely—about 1 hour—before proceeding.

Ahead-of-Time Note: The cake may be baked several days in advance. Wrap airtight in plastic wrap, return it to the bowl, and refrigerate.

Melting the Chocolate: Bring 2 inches of water to a simmer in the 8-inch saucepan, set the bowl over it, add 5 ounces of chocolate, and remove from heat. When completely melted and smooth, remove the bowl from over the water and let cool to room temperature.

Whipping the Cream: Whip the cream to soft peaks in a bowl set over a larger bowl of ice cubes and water.

Combining Cream and Chocolate: Fold half of the cream into the cooled but liquid chocolate; when incorporated, fold in the rest to complete the mousse.

Assembling the Cake: Taste the orange juice, adding a little sugar if needed, and, if you wish, 2 tablespoonfuls of Grand Marnier or orange

INGREDIENTS FOR 8 SERVINGS

For the cake-baking bowl
1 tablespoon of soft unsalted butter
Several tablespoons of flour
4 "large" eggs
1 cup granulated sugar
¾ cup plain bleached cake flour, in a sifter
11–12 ounces of top-quality semisweet (bittersweet) chocolate, 5 ounces for filling, 6–7 ounces for coating and decoration
1 cup chilled heavy cream
1 cup fresh-squeezed orange juice, sweetened to taste
2 tablespoons Grand Marnier or excellent orange liqueur (optional)
1 pint fresh red raspberries

(continued)

The Chocolate Dome (continued)

For decoration

The melted chocolate

*6 to 8 fresh green leaves, such
as orange, lemon, or bay*

*1 tablespoon cocoa powder in
a very fine meshed sieve*

2 cups raspberry sauce

RASPBERRY SAUCE

1-½ cups fresh raspberries
½ cup or more sugar
2 tablespoons fresh lemon juice

Puree the raspberries with ½ cup sugar in a blender or processor. Add the lemon juice, taste, and adjust the flavor if necessary. Push the sauce through a fine sieve. Makes 2 cups.

liqueur. Use a serrated knife to slice the Génoise horizontally into three layers of equal thickness. Shave off and discard the crusty top of the cake—it will be too firm to absorb the liquid to come. Line the same 8-inch baking bowl with a piece of plastic wrap. Fit the rounded top piece of cake into the lined bowl. Using a pastry brush, soak the cake with about 4 tablespoons of the orange juice mixture. Spoon ⅓ of the chocolate mousse onto the soaked cake layer, and strew on a small handful of raspberries.

Place the next layer of cake onto the first, brush with ⅓ cup of the orange juice mixture, spoon on the rest of the mousse, a handful of raspberries, and cover with the remaining slice of cake. Brush on the last of the juice, and bring the hanging edges of the plastic wrap over the top. Cover with another sheet of plastic, and refrigerate for several hours before decorating.

Note: Cake may be assembled to this point a day in advance.

Making the Chocolate Icing: Melt the remaining choco-

late in a bowl set over simmering water, as you did for the mousse. Remove the plastic covering from the cake bowl and fold back the plastic that is covering the cake. Unmold the thoroughly chilled cake, domed side up, onto a rack, then peel off and discard the rest of the plastic covering. Lightly dampen your work surface so that a sheet of plastic wrap will adhere, and lay out a 12-inch sheet. Using a rubber spatula, spread a thin 10–11-inch disk of cool liquid chocolate in the center of the sheet. Rapidly slide the plastic into the bowl, letting the plastic with its chocolate disk cover the bottom and sides of the bowl. Gently drop the chilled cake, domed side down, into the bowl, fold the plastic wrap over it, and refrigerate.

Making the Chocolate Leaves: Dip the inside of each leaf into the remaining melted chocolate and place on a plate, coated side up. Refrigerate until the chocolate hardens.

Decorating the Cake: Remove the cake from the refrigerator and again fold back the plastic wrap. Turn the cake domed side up onto a serving platter and lift off the plastic to reveal a beautifully smooth, shiny chocolate surface. Sprinkle with a dusting of cocoa powder. Make a ring of raspberries around the edge of the cake and pour a little of the raspberry sauce over them. Remove the chocolate leaves from the refrigerator. Gently separate the green leaves from the chocolate ones, then one by one dip the stem of each into melted chocolate and gently affix it near the center of the cake, making an upstanding bouquet of 4 or 5 leaves as illustrated. Decorate with a few strategically placed raspberries.

Ahead-of-Time Note: May be finished and refrigerated several hours in advance of serving. Let set at room temperature for an hour before serving so that the chocolate will lose its rigidity.

Serving the Chocolate Dome: At the table, provide yourself with a tall decorative pitcher of hot water, a long sharp knife, and a napkin. Dip the knife in the hot water and wipe it off with the napkin before every cut. Surround each serving with a handful of raspberries covered with a spoonful of raspberry sauce.

SPECIAL EQUIPMENT SUGGESTED

A pastry brush
A 4-cup stainless steel bowl about 8 inches across and 3 inches deep, for baking the cake
An efficient electric mixer
A large rubber spatula
Plastic wrap
For chocolate melting: An 8-inch saucepan and a stainless steel bowl that fits snugly over it (see page 61)
A metal bowl and whisk for whipping cream
A serrated knife for cutting cake into layers

Hot Chocolate Truffles

Chocolate truffles are ever popular as an indulgent snack or the sweet finish to a meal, but traditionally they are a cold mouthful. Michel Richard introduces the hot truffle—not burning hot, just a warm mouthful of melted chocolate encased in a sweet crusty shell. These are not items for mass cooking, and they need careful last-minute attention—you pass them around on a linen-draped silver platter, one or two to a few special guests at the end of a splendid dinner.

INGREDIENTS FOR 3-½ TO 4 DOZEN TRUFFLES

For the chocolate ganache
1 pound semisweet chocolate,
see important note on
chocolate on opposite page
1 cup of hot whipping cream

For frying the truffles
Peanut oil

Making the Ganache: Melt the chocolate over hot water as described in the previous recipe (page 61). Stir the chocolate until it is completely smooth, then stir in the cream. Remove the chocolate pan from the water pan and let set for half an hour, then cover and refrigerate until chilled.

Forming the Truffles: Scoop out 1-tablespoon gobs of chocolate with the melon baller and roll in the palms of your hands to make balls 1 inch in diameter. Arrange the balls on parchment-lined cookie sheets and place in the freezer for 1-½ hours.

Coating the Truffles: Prepare the "coating station" with plates of flour, the eggs, and crumbs (page 65). Remove the chocolate balls from the freezer, and roll 4 at a time in the flour, then roll one at a time in the palms of your hands. Next, roll them in the beaten eggs, coating them completely.

Finally, roll them in the crumb mixture, coating them completely, and then one by one roll them firmly in the palms of your hands so that the crumbs will stick well to the chocolate and the balls will be perfectly round. Repeat the process, rolling first in flour, then egg, and finally crumbs. Arrange them again on the parchment-lined pans and freeze for an hour.

Ahead-of-Time Note: Cover if you are leaving them longer and they will keep for several weeks.

Frying the Truffles: Heat the peanut oil in the heavy saucepan to 350° F —a piece of bread will brown lightly at that temperature in 8 to 10 seconds. Lower 4 truffles at a time into the hot oil; let brown and crust for about 10 seconds, then drain on paper towels.

Important Note on Chocolate: You will have best results with the "couverture" chocolate that Michel uses, and you'll usually find it only in specialty stores or some of the mail-order houses. Although you can use regular semisweet supermarket chocolate, it is usually softer and fattier than the professional couverture, and you may have trouble with the truffles cracking or leaking.

Serving the Truffles: If you are serving only a favored few and can do so almost immediately, the truffles will be sweetly crusty on the outside with a thick layer of warm chocolate contrasting dramatically with an inner nugget of cool chocolate. For a larger group—more than two dozen guests, however, may well result in a severe drop in quality—place the truffles in a 300° F oven for 3 to 4 minutes. Serve immediately and tell your guests to pop them into their mouths whole—otherwise the melted chocolate will spill.

COOK'S NOTES

FOR THE COATING STATION

2 cups sifted flour on a plate

3 eggs beaten with a pinch of salt in a wide bowl

The crumb mixture on a plate:
  1-½ cups fine white bread crumbs
  1-½ cups sugar
  ¼ to ⅓ cup cinnamon

SPECIAL EQUIPMENT SUGGESTED

The chocolate-melting setup (page 63)

A melon baller with 1-inch bowl

Several cookie sheets lined with parchment paper

An electric blender for bread crumbs

A heavy 2-quart pan for the frying oil

A skimmer for removing the truffles

Amy Ferguson-Ota

The Ritz-Carlton, Mauna Lani, Hawaii

my Ferguson-Ota has the wind at her back and the "tu-tus" by her side. This sparkling young executive chef at the Ritz-Carlton, Mauna Lani on Hawaii, is the first woman ever appointed to this demanding position by this luxury hotel group. Amy's enticing and multi-faceted cooking blends the cuisine of her native Texas with classic French and that of her adopted Big Island home. The "tu-tus," or island elders, have helped her do that by showing her how to search at dawn to find the finest pohole ferns for her salads or to wait until after a tropical rainstorm to pick the freshest thimbleberries. "You learn from the elders—or by accident. The first time I picked up a taro leaf, I ate a piece and had a rash for three days! I'm lucky, though—my husband, Frank, is a second-generation Hawaiian equipped with elders, too."

Chef Amy has been smitten with food for as long as she can remember. As a little girl she spent carefree afternoons cooking with her Creole grandmother from Louisiana. Amy pursued art history and French studies in France so she could hang out at food markets, take courses at Le Cordon Bleu, and more or less absorb cooking.

By the time she returned to Houston she was determined to find work in the food profession. She was teaching French cooking classes when her brother told her about Che, a new restaurant opening in Houston. For three weeks, Amy chased down the owner, Tom Emeric, until he finally gave her a job. "He hammered me into shape," says Amy, who went on to be one of the youngest executive chefs at other acclaimed Texas restaurants.

"Aloha" takes on a special meaning for those who dine at any one of the four hotel restaurants that Chef Amy oversees, and we are delighted with the feeling of Hawaii she brings us—fresh tuna cakes with breadfruit, tangy papaya, wok-seared ono (all are doable here).

Ahi Yellowfin Tuna and Ulu Breadfruit Cakes with Lime-Cilantro Mayonnaise

On a trip to the mainland, Amy Ferguson-Ota noticed that everyone everywhere was serving crab cakes, the trendy food of the moment. When she returned to Hawaii, she decided to be trendy, too, but in a Hawaiian way. Her tasty local version uses "ahi"—fresh yellowfin tuna, while "ulu," Hawaiian breadfruit, takes the place of the usual bread crumbs or potatoes, and here, sweet potatoes may replace breadfruit. Serve these for lunch, brunch, or supper, and you could accompany them with her green papaya salad and a chilled dry white wine.

Steaming the Breadfruit (or Taro or Sweet Potato): Cut the breadfruit in half through the stem; peel the halves, slice out the cores, and steam 20 minutes or so until almost tender—they get more cooking later. (Or, steam a sweet potato the same way.) Put through the coarse holes of the grater and set aside.

Sautéing the Tuna: Slice the tuna ⅜-inch thick, then into ⅜-inch strips, and then into cubes. Heat 2 tablespoons of clarified butter in the pan, stir in the diced onion, shallot, and garlic, and cook, stirring for several minutes until translucent. Then add the tuna, stirring and tossing for several minutes, and sprinkling on a little salt. The tuna is done when barely springy to the touch. Set aside in a bowl and chill.

Forming the Cakes: Blend the tuna and breadfruit in a large bowl with the cilantro, cornstarch, baking powder, and egg. Then add small spoonfuls of cream to soften the mixture enough for easy forming with your hands. Taste, then season carefully with lemon juice, salt, and pepper.

TUNA TALK

Fresh tuna is extremely expensive, over $20 a pound in some instances. The highest and most expensive and luxurious grade, No. 1, is eaten raw as sashimi. No. 2, the middle grade, can be for sashimi but is especially for steaks and cooked recipes. No. 3, the belly part, has more sinews and is for stews and ground meat.

INGREDIENTS FOR TWELVE 3-INCH CAKES

1 pound ulu (breadfruit) or Chinese taro or sweet potato

The fish

1 pound fresh tuna, No. 2 quality (see box: Tuna Talk)

2 tablespoons clarified butter (see box, page 68)

1 medium-sized mild onion (Maui, or vidalia type, if possible), peeled and diced

1 large shallot, peeled and diced

2 large cloves garlic, peeled, smashed, and minced

Salt to taste

(continued)

Ahi Yellowfin Tuna (continued)

Remaining ingredients for the cakes

Small handful of cilantro (leaves and tender stems), chopped

6 fine fresh scallions (both white and fresh green), chopped

⅓ cup cornstarch

1 tablespoon baking powder

1 "large" egg

½ to ¾ cup heavy cream

2 tablespoons fresh lemon juice

Salt and pepper to taste

3 tablespoons or more clarified butter

For the lime-cilantro mayonnaise

1-½ cups top-quality mayonnaise whisked with:

3 tablespoons fresh lime juice

2 tablespoons fresh chopped cilantro

Salt and freshly ground white pepper

SPECIAL EQUIPMENT SUGGESTED

A very sharp slicing knife

A Chinese bamboo steamer setup, or a steamer basket set in a saucepan with tight-fitting cover

A grater with coarse holes, or a food processor with coarse-holed disk

A 10-inch, no-stick sauté pan

Scoop out large spoonfuls of the mixture and shape in the palms of your hands into fish cakes any size you wish.

Ahead-of-Time Note: May be made to this point and refrigerated for several hours.

Cooking and Serving the Tuna Cakes: Mix together the ingredients for the lime-cilantro mayonnaise. When ready to serve, heat 3 tablespoons of clarified butter in the sauté pan and cook the cakes for several minutes on each side to heat through and brown nicely. Drain on paper towel before transferring to serving plates. Accompany with the lime-cilantro mayonnaise, and garnish with the following papaya salad or sliced limes and fresh cilantro.

CLARIFIED BUTTER

Chef Amy's Hawaiian cooking style does not call for a great deal of butter, but she has no hesitation when she needs it, especially for sautés calling for clarified butter. "There is no substitute for the taste of good butter," says she emphatically.

All butter contains a small percentage of milk residue. It is this residue that not only turns butter rancid but burns and blackens when butter is overheated. To clear the butter, you can either melt it and pour the clear yellow liquid off the residue or you can use the following professional method (since butter keeps for months when fully clarified this way, it may be worth your while to prepare a whole pound while you are at it): Dice the butter and melt it in a fairly large pan over moderately high heat. Keep a close eye on it from now on: after a few minutes of boiling, it will start sputtering and crackling as the milky residue evaporates. When the crackling begins to subside, clarification is almost complete, and when it suddenly foams up it is done. At once, remove the butter from heat or it will burn and blacken. Pour the clear yellow liquid through a tea strainer into a preserving jar, leaving any dark brown speckles of residue behind. As the butter cools and congeals, the color will change from yellow to cream. Cover and store in the refrigerator, or you may freeze it.

Puna Green Papaya Salad with Spicy Dressing

It looks like a finely shredded coleslaw, and like coleslaw it can be eaten with almost anything. A most unusual salad, its principal ingredient, green papaya, gives it a fresh, spritely, lightly spicy taste. Created by Chef Amy, this is a thoroughly Hawaiian dish that goes beautifully with her tuna cakes, as well as with grilled fish or chicken, pork chops, and rice and lentil dishes.

PAPAYA TALK

More than fifty varieties of papaya exist in the world, and of them all Chef Amy prefers the so-called strawberry papaya because of its reddish flesh and sweetness. The one most common in our markets, however, is the deep yellow "puna" variety. A ripe papaya yields to gentle pressure, and its flesh has the consistency rather like that of a ripe pear. Cut it open lengthwise: the seeds appear to be a dense nest of damp black peppercorns, and indeed they are peppery. Chef Amy makes a sauce of them, as described on the next page. The green papayas which concern us here have gray or almost white, quite flavorless seeds, the flesh is hard and crisp with its own special taste of green apples with a faintly peppery overtone.

Preparing the Dressing: Measure the dressing ingredients into a screw-cap jar, shake vigorously, taste carefully for seasoning, screw on the lid, and set aside.

PAPAYA SEED SAUCE:

Scrape the black seeds from a ripe papaya into the bowl of a blender or food processor, adding the flesh of ½ avocado and/or mango and ½ papaya. Add about ¼ cup of wine vinegar, several tablespoons of Dijon-type mustard, ½ cup vegetable oil (not olive), a little honey, and a bit of salt to taste (no pepper needed!). Serve with pork, duck, broiled or grilled fish, or use it as a marinade for chicken.

INGREDIENTS FOR 8 OR MORE SERVINGS

For the dressing
⅓ cup lime juice
¼ cup sugar
¼ cup oriental fish sauce (or 1 teaspoon soy sauce to taste)
2 teaspoons Chinese chili sauce (or 1 or 2 red jalapeño peppers with seeds, finely chopped)

(continued)

Papaya Salad (continued)

For the salad

2 small or 1 large green (unripe) papayas

4 ripe red medium-sized tomatoes

1 small red chili pepper, finely sliced (optional)

½ teaspoon freshly grated ginger

2 scallions, chopped

Medium handful of cilantro (leaves and tender stems), chopped

SPECIAL EQUIPMENT SUGGESTED

A grater with very fine holes for the papaya

A 2-quart salad bowl

A ginger grater is useful

Preparing the Salad Ingredients:

The Papaya. Using a vegetable peeler, remove the skin from the papaya, slice the fruit in half lengthwise, scoop out and discard the seeds (you will have to scrape hard with green papaya). Cut the fruit into very fine julienne strips using a mandoline (see page 138), and place in bowl.

The Tomatoes. To blanch the tomatoes, drop them into a pan of boiling water for 10 seconds, which loosens the skin. Cut out the core, strip off the skin, quarter through the stem, then halve the quarters into wedges. Lay each wedge flat on your work surface and slide a knife under the pulp and seeds to remove them. Finally, cut the remaining flesh into julienne strips and place in bowl.

Hot Pepper. To avoid irritating her skin while handling hot peppers, Chef Amy oils her hands. And if she wants maximum heat, she leaves the seeds in. But for this recipe, she slices the pepper in half lengthwise, scrapes out the seeds with her fingers, and cuts the seeded pepper halves into julienne strips. These, too, place in the bowl. (See notes on peppers, page 78.)

Final Touches: Add the ginger, scallions, and cilantro to the bowl. First toss the salad to mix the ingredients, then toss with spoonfuls of dressing (Chef Amy uses chopsticks). Carefully correct seasoning. You may serve it immediately, but waiting half an hour will allow the flavors to blend.

Ahead-of-Time Note: Keeps nicely for 2 or 3 days in the refrigerator.

Serving the Papaya Salad: To serve with tuna cakes, for example, place a small serving of salad in the middle of the plate and a tuna cake at each side with a dollop of lime-cilantro mayonnaise on top. Garnish with a few fresh sprigs of cilantro, perhaps setting an edible flower to one side.

Wok-Seared Ono and Steamed Banana

Fresh fish steaks, seared medium rare and served with a spicy banana curry and honeyed whole bananas steamed in Hawaiian "ti" leaves, indeed is a dish that speaks of the very essence of Hawaii, and one that would star on any menu for lunch, brunch, or dinner.

FISH TALK

"Ono" is a mild, close-grained, white-fleshed Hawaiian fish, known in Florida as "wahoo." Chef Amy says you can use any fish that can stand up to searing and enjoys being associated with bananas but she especially recommends swordfish steaks since they have much the same texture and taste as ono.

SPEAKING OF TI LEAVES

Ti leaves are 18 inches or longer, tapering from a narrow stem and tip to a general width of 6 inches. They grow wild in Hawaiian gardens, and everyone uses them as food wrappers, storers, and servers, as well as for table decorations. They are the Hawaiian aluminum foil. Florists have ti leaves but they are expensive and often sprayed. In place of wrapping and steaming the bananas, bake them according to the directions in the recipe.

(continued)

GINGER FACTS

Use only very fresh, firm, unwithered ginger. Wrapped airtight and refrigerated, it will keep for several weeks. Peel before using and use freshly grated ginger almost at once, since its flavor and aroma are fleeting. Peel ginger with the tip of a teaspoon; Chef Amy has a special metal ginger grater "used by everyone here on the islands," wherein one rubs the peeled ginger over a grating screen and the juices fall into a trough at the bottom.

If you live in the right climate, you can grow your own ginger. Simply cut off the little knobs and plant them, cut end up and just uncovered, in your garden. Don't throw out the skin: chop it up and let it infuse in a bottle of oil for a week or two and you have your own "private" ginger oil. Use it for sautéing fish, flavoring vegetables and chicken, and so forth.

Wok-Seared Ono (continued)

(continued)

INGREDIENTS FOR 6 SERVINGS

For the cinnamon-lemon oil (to be made in advance)

½ cup vegetable oil

1 lemon

2 large cinnamon sticks

For pre-seasoning the fish

The above cinnamon-lemon oil

Salt

Ground pepper

Toasted coriander, ground (see page 136)

For the banana curry

1 teaspoon olive oil

1 large garlic clove

1 large shallot, chopped

1 teaspoon or more fragrant curry powder or Thai curry paste

5 large ripe bananas, peeled and coarsely chopped

¼ cup chicken broth

¼ teaspoon fresh-squeezed lemon juice

Salt and pepper

1 teaspoon sushi vinegar (rice vinegar) or white wine vinegar

A little honey (if needed)

The Cinnamon-Lemon Oil: Mix the oil with the juice of 1 lemon and cinnamon sticks in a bowl. Cover and let steep for several hours or overnight.

Seasoning the Fish: An hour or so before cooking, brush the fish with the cinnamon-lemon oil and season with salt, pepper, and toasted coriander. Cover and refrigerate.

The Banana Curry: Heat the oil in the sauté pan, stir in the garlic, shallot, and curry and cook over moderately low heat for a minute or two, and then add the chopped bananas and chicken broth. Cook over moderately high heat, stirring frequently, for 5 minutes or more, until the bananas are soft but not mushy. Using a spoon or potato masher to break the bananas up, continue to cook until they form a thick, rather rough puree. Season to your taste with lemon juice, salt, pepper, droplets of vinegar, and even a little honey if the bananas are not sweet enough. Banana curry should have a distinct personality and a nice balance of sweet and sour, banana, curry, and spice. Scrape into a bowl; it will thicken as it cools.

Steaming or Baking the Bananas: Place a ti leaf shiny side down on your work surface, center a banana lengthwise upon it, and spread with the honey-cinnamon nut mixture. Fold the two long sides of the leaf over the banana, then the two ends, leaving half an inch of leaf tip protruding from the package. Continue with the rest. Prepare the steamer, place the banana packages in it, and steam for 20 minutes or so until the bananas

HOW TO USE TI LEAVES

Ti leaves must be stemmed and made pliable if you use them as wrappers. To stem a leaf, turn it shiny side down and feel the stem, which hardens and thickens at its base and thins out near the tip. Locate a spot about a third of the way down where you can definitely feel stem. Nick that portion with a knife, just to break through the leaf covering, then bend the leaf back to break the stem at that point while at the same time exposing a portion of broken stem. Holding the bottom part of the leaf in one hand, strip the leaf from the stem with the other. It looks easy indeed when Chef Amy does it, but stemming is a knack: if your initial nick is too deep, the two sides of the leaf separate; if too shallow, you are not getting down to the stem. (The best way to learn is to take a working vacation in Hawaii, where the ti leaves grow wild.) After stemming, and again to achieve more pliability, heat a burner on the stove and pass the flat side of each leaf rather slowly over it. They are now ready as wrappers.

are just tender but not mushy—do not overcook or they will be difficult to serve—carefully opening one to see. Alternately, arrange the peeled bananas in a buttered baking dish; coat with the honey, cinnamon, and nuts, and bake 15 to 20 minutes at 400° F. Keep warm while cooking the fish.

Searing the Fish: Heat the wok(s) or sauté pan(s)—they need no oil since the fish was oiled—and when very hot, lay in the fish. Sear on one side for a minute or two, turn and sear on the other until nicely brown. The fish is done when it just begins to feel springy rather than squashy to the touch—the outside is brown and crisp, the inside medium rare.

Serving the Fish and Bananas: Center the fish on a hot plate. Cut the banana packages in half on the diagonal and prop one half against the other to one side of the plate. Spoon banana curry next to it and decorate with crossed cinnamon sticks. Decorate attractively with whatever you have chosen—Chef Amy suggests fresh mint leaves and Hawaiian red torch ginger flowers for a very pretty motif. Serve at once.

For the steamed bananas

6 fresh green ti leaves (see box, page 72)

6 "finger" or "apple" bananas about 4 inches long, peeled, or 3 regular bananas peeled and cut in half

Blend in a bowl: ¼ cup honey, ½ teaspoon powdered cinnamon, ½ cup roughly ground macadamia nuts

The fish and the finish

6 portions of fine very fresh fish, 6 to 7 ounces each (see Fish Talk at beginning of recipe)

Cinnamon sticks, sprigs of greenery, edible flowers

SPECIAL EQUIPMENT SUGGESTED

A 10-inch, no-stick sauté pan

A Chinese bamboo steamer setup, or a steamer basket set in a roomy saucepan with tight-fitting cover

A well-seasoned wok or two, or no-stick sauté pans

Robert Del Grande

Café Annie, Houston

In 1981, Robert Del Grande was visiting his future wife, Mimi, in Houston, Texas, where her sister and brother-in-law owned a small bistro. Their chef's abrupt departure had left the year-old Café Annie without a leader in the kitchen. Robert had no formal culinary training, but he helped out and the results were so successful, he's been there ever since.

He was not a stranger to the food business; he had worked as a teenager in San Francisco in an ice-cream parlor where after a few months he was running the show. However, Robert pursued a degree not in food but in biochemistry and holds a doctorate degree. He has applied his academic training to his adopted profession. "It's not as important to know the information as to know where to find it."

When he realized his temporary position held a future, he asked questions of everyone and read cookbooks, voraciously winding his way from basic techniques to ethnic influences. When he opened his more casual bistro, Rio Ranch, ten years later, he was still asking. He wanted to serve the extremely popular home-style dish chicken-fried steak, so he asked chefs, grandmothers, and neighbors for their recipes. "If you ask, you'll get miles instead of walking in circles with your eyes closed." Robert obviously asked the right questions because his chicken-fried steak is one of the most popular items on the menu.

The thirty-eight-year-old chef is fascinated with what happens to the flavors of ingredients under a variety of conditions. "On an everyday basis we don't use a huge variety of ingredients but a core of foods treated under a variety of conditions to create new dishes—which is why we can eat substantially better than animals." He illustrates his points well and deliciously in two recipes he has given us, one for seared scallops with a spicy sauce, and the other for tenderloin steaks, again in one of his unique sauces.

Fresh Corn Pudding

Robert Del Grande's tender and naturally sweet corn pudding goes beautifully with seared scallops, or could be served with roast chicken or ham, or as part of a vegetable plate, or with breakfast eggs, and so forth. It is a very simple natural formula of cornmeal, boiling milk, and grated fresh corn—taking but a few minutes to make once the corn is grated.

Note: Unless you know your cornmeal, it is best to make and serve promptly—some cornmeals, according to Chef Robert, have more binding qualities than others, meaning they can stand and wait while some thin out if held.

Preparing the Fresh Corn: Husk the corn and rub the kernels through the large holes of a grater, pushing hard on the cob as you grate to bring out all the "milk." You should have about 1 cup of creamy corn puree—this can be done somewhat ahead, covered, and refrigerated.

Making the Pudding: Bring the milk to the boil with the salt. Slowly and steadily whisk in the cornmeal, beating thoroughly to avoid lumps. Then stir with a wooden spoon over moderately low heat, until the mixture thickens. Stir in the corn puree and the mixture will thicken more—which happens quickly. Stir in the cream, and serve at once.

INGREDIENTS FOR 4 TO 6 SERVINGS

For the corn
4 to 5 ears of fresh corn

For the pudding mixture
2 cups milk
½ teaspoon salt
½ cup cornmeal

For serving
2 tablespoons heavy cream

Sea Scallops with Wild Mushrooms in Green Sauce

A small serving of tender sweet sea scallops nestled on a bed of creamy corn pudding is an inviting appetizer or luncheon dish, while a larger portion makes a colorful and satisfying main course. The sauce—a combination of citrusy tomatillos, sharp serrano chiles, and woodsy wild mushrooms—is a delicate balance of flavors.

In this recipe and the following one for beef tenderloin steaks, Chef Robert uses a technique that Mexicans call "frying the sauce." He deglazes; that is, he gathers all the caramelized flavors of his pan-seared scallops by pouring a cool sauce into the hot pan and boiling up the flavors.

INGREDIENTS FOR 6 FIRST-COURSE SERVINGS

For the tomatillo puree
*1 stemmed serrano chile,
    whole, or halved lengthwise
    and seeded (more
    information on page 78)
1 pound tomatillos, husked
    and stemmed
½ large white onion, peeled
    and coarsely chopped
2 large peeled garlic cloves*

For the mushroom sauce
*4 tablespoons softened
    unsalted butter (2 for the
    mushrooms, 2 for the
    scallops)
8 ounces shiitake mushrooms
    (or other wild mushrooms),
    wiped clean and cut in
    large pieces
½ cup chicken stock (a little
    more if needed)
1 teaspoon salt
Pinch of sugar if necessary to
    balance the tartness of the
    tomatillos*

(continued)

Sea Scallops (continued)

Manufacturing Note: Pan-searing is most successful with a large skillet, since each scallop needs airspace around it so it will brown rather than steam. Therefore, the wider the better, and the recipe here serves 6 as a first course: 2 jumbo scallops apiece (or 3 or 4 normal-sized ones).

Preparing the Tomatillo Puree: Place the chile, tomatillos, onion, and garlic, in a 2-quart saucepan and add just enough water to cover the ingredients; the tomatillos should bob around a bit. Bring to the simmer for about 10 minutes; the tomatillos should remain whole, and will plump and feel soft, but don't overcook them.

Immediately drain off the liquid and transfer the vegetables to a blender or processor. Process for several seconds only, to form a coarse puree. Set aside.

Preparing the Mushroom Sauce:

Sautéing the Mushrooms. Melt two tablespoons of butter in a sauté pan over moderately high heat. When the butter is hot and beginning to brown, stir in the mushrooms. Sauté until lightly browned, and bits of caramelized juices appear in the pan—almost 10 minutes of fairly frequent tossing and stirring.

Finishing the Sauce. Stir the tomatillo puree into the mushrooms and "fry the sauce" over high heat, stirring all over the bottom of the pan with a wooden spoon for about 2 minutes. Pour in enough chicken stock to make a saucelike consistency, and bring to the simmer. Taste carefully for seasoning, adding salt as necessary, and a pinch of sugar if the sauce seems too tart. Simmer for 8 to 10 minutes to blend flavors; correct seasoning again.

Ahead-of-Time Note: May be prepared to this point several hours in advance.

Sautéing the Scallops: Lightly salt and pepper the scallops. Set the frying pan over high heat, add the remaining 2 tablespoons of butter. When the bubbling has begun to subside, rapidly arrange the scallops in the pan, leaving ½ inch between each—it is important that they do not touch (see page 135 for more on pan-searing).

When they are nicely browned on both sides, reduce the heat to moderately high and continue to sauté the scallops for a few minutes, turning now and then, with your tongs.

When Are They Done? When you press them with your finger and squeeze them gently, they should feel lightly springy, fairly firm, but with a little bit of give—opaque outside and translucent inside.

Serving: Quickly reheat the sauce and stir in the cilantro. Place a scoop of warm corn pudding in the center of each dinner plate. Spoon some of the wild mushroom sauce over the pudding and around the plate. Arrange the scallops on top of the pudding and drizzle a bit of cream around the scallops and over the sauce. Top the scallops with a spoonful of tomato salsa, decorate with a sprig of cilantro, and serve.

For the scallops

8 ounces large, fine, very fresh sea scallops, hard white nubbin around circumference removed

Salt

Freshly ground pepper

For serving

A small handful fresh cilantro, chopped (plus whole sprigs for garnish)

Fresh corn pudding (preceding recipe)

¼ cup heavy cream

Fresh tomato salsa (see page 81)

SPECIAL EQUIPMENT SUGGESTED

An electric blender or food processor

A heavy-duty 12-inch frying pan

Tongs

Warmed dinner plates

CHILES

Chiles! A symbol of Texas and at the heart of the region's cooking. With a diversity of shapes, types, and flavors, chiles are fascinating, but with the proliferation of names they are also confusing. Chef Robert suggests that in making a selection, you concentrate less on the names and more on the characteristics of the various peppers. Chef Robert prepared the following outline for us.

I. **Two Basic Categories of Chiles**
   a. Fresh green chiles
      unripened fruit-type flavors
   b. Dried red chiles
      flavors ranging from ripe chile flavors to dried fruit flavors. A good example is the contrast between green and red bell peppers.
   c. With one minor lacuna
      1. green chiles ripen to red: therefore fresh red chiles. A large variety of fresh red chiles is not widely available.
      2. Some varieties are, however, commercially available; e.g., jalapeños, serranos, fresnos, big jim chiles, et cetera.

II. **Naming Chiles; Two Categories of Names—Green vs. Red**
   a. Chiles in the green form have a specific name
   b. When red and dried, the chile has a different name
   c. For example: poblano (green) changes to ancho (red)
      chilaca (green) changes to pasilla (dark brown)

III. **Two Extremes That Help Indicate Level of Spice**
   (this applies to both green and red chiles)
   a. Very small relates to very spicy
   b. Very large or long relates to mild
   c. As with most of nature, wide variations can occur; e.g., very large and spicy

IV. **Testing or Tasting for Spice Levels**
   a. For green chiles: Cut chile in half lengthwise to expose seed pod. Smell seed pod. A tingling sensation in your nose or the sharp smell of spice indicates very spicy. Alternatively, taste a thin slice of chile near the seed pod (the tip of the chile distel from the stem is rarely very spicy). The level of spice will probably be obvious. To reduce the level of spice, remove the seed pod.
   b. For dried red chiles: Because the seed pod is now dried, its spicy oil has spread throughout the chile. Therefore, you'll have to taste a small piece to judge the heat, but make sure it is *very* small if you are uncertain as to how volatile the chile may be.

V. **Two Classes of Dried Red Chiles**
   a. Smooth, thin-skinned chiles: ripe chile flavor but not sweet or fruity. These chiles do not tend to produce a thick sauce. A good example is a dried New Mexican red chile.
   b. Wrinkled, thick-skinned chiles: sweeter with the flavor of dried fruit such as raisins, prunes or other dried fruits. These chiles produce a thick, rich sauce. A good example is an Ancho Chile.

Be very careful handling any hot chiles because once the spicy oils get on your fingers, if you so much as touch your eye, you will be in pain. (Amy Ferguson-Ota always oils her hands before working with chiles.)

Filets of Beef in Pasilla Chile Sauce

Beef and chiles—two Texas staples—Robert Del Grande brings them together in this recipe for seared filet mignon steaks braised in a Texas-style tomato and chile sauce. The chiles are long dark brown ones called pasilla, which he first "toasts" in a dry pan, to release their deep earthy, mushroomy flavor. Chef Robert tastes carefully as he cooks, and out of season he will often add brown sugar or molasses to his tomato sauces, to balance the acidity of the tomatoes and to bring out a hint of Texas barbecue.

For a contrast of temperatures and textures, he tops the warm dish with a cool mound of fresh, tart avocado relish, and a sprinkling of grated Cotija—Mexican cow's-milk cheese with a mild, tangy flavor—for which out-of-staters could substitute aged, dried feta cheese.

Toasting the Chiles: Set the small frying pan over moderate heat, and when hot add the chiles. Toast for 5 minutes or so, turning a few times—you will know they are done when you can smell their heady aroma. Let cool briefly, then remove and discard the stems. Pull the peppers apart lengthwise with your fingers; scoop out and discard the seeds. Break into large pieces.

Preparing the Sauce: Turn the broiler on high, and arrange the tomatoes, onion, and garlic in the large frying pan. Set the pan about 3 inches from the hot broiler element, and let the vegetables brown and blister, shaking the pan occasionally, for about about 15 minutes. Cool slightly, then scrape into the blender or food processor.

Pour the chicken stock into the pan, scraping into it any coagulated juices, then pour this liquid into the blender. Add the toasted chiles and process for 5 to 10 seconds, until the mixture is a coarse puree with some small lumps. Set aside.

INGREDIENTS FOR 4 SERVINGS

For the chile sauce
2 pasilla chiles (2 ounces)
6 ripe plum tomatoes
½ large white onion, peeled and coarsely chopped
3 peeled garlic cloves
1 cup chicken stock

For the beef
4 beef tenderloin steaks (filet mignons), 6 ounces each, perfectly trimmed, leaving just the thick round of meat
Salt
Freshly ground black pepper
1 tablespoon peanut oil (or olive oil)

(continued)

Filets of Beef (continued)

For final flavoring and serving

2 teaspoons brown sugar

A small handful of fresh cilantro

⅔ cup avocado relish (see page 81)

¼ cup grated Cotija cheese (or dried feta cheese)

SPECIAL EQUIPMENT SUGGESTED

A small frying pan

A heavy-duty, 10-inch frying pan (or 2 frying pans)

An electric blender or food processor

Tongs

Searing the Steaks: Just before cooking the steaks, dry them thoroughly in paper towels; salt and pepper generously on both sides. Wash out and dry the frying pan, or use the second pan; set over moderately high heat. When very hot, add the oil. Lay the steaks in the pan and sear one side a few minutes until a nice crust forms. Turn with your tongs, sear the other side, and remove to a side dish—they will cook more later with the sauce. (See page 135 for more on pan-searing.)

Finishing the Sauce: Pour any cooking oil out of the hot frying pan, pour in the sauce, and "fry it"; that is, stirring with a wooden spoon and reaching all over the bottom of the pan, bringing the sauce to the boil, scraping into it all the caramelized meat juices. Taste for seasoning, adding a little salt, pepper, and sugar as needed—do not exaggerate, since it will get more seasoning later. Lower heat and simmer for 20 minutes. If the sauce becomes too thick, add spoonfuls of water.

Ahead-of-Time Note: Steaks and sauce may be completed an hour or so in advance.

Finishing the Steaks: Keeping the sauce at the barest simmer, add the cilantro and place the steaks in the warm sauce. Without letting it boil, almost continuously spoon the sauce over the meat as it reheats—3 to 5 minutes for medium rare—and keep testing by pressing the meat with your finger, as the chefs do (see page 135). Taste the sauce carefully, and correct seasoning.

Serving Filets of Beef in Pasilla Chile Sauce: Place a steak in the center of each dinner plate and spoon some sauce over the meat. Spoon a few tablespoons of avocado relish on top, and finish with a light sprinkling of grated cheese over all.

Two Southwest Relishes

Cool relishes on top of hot dishes are a good example of one of the ways Chef Robert enjoys experimenting with temperatures. He is so fond of creating contrasts that his staff claims that if they don't serve a dish the minute it is finished he just continues to add to it.

The fresh, subtly spicy relishes below are two he uses often. Make them within a few hours of their use or they will look and taste tired.

AVOCADO RELISH

Cut the avocados in half, remove the pits, and cut into fine dice. Turn into a small bowl and fold in the remaining ingredients. Taste carefully and correct seasoning.

Ahead-of-Time Note: If not used almost immediately, turn into a bowl, film top with olive oil, and cover with plastic wrap. Will store at room temperature for an hour or two.

INGREDIENTS FOR 2-½ CUPS

2 medium-sized avocados
(Haas variety suggested)
½ red bell pepper, stemmed,
seeded, and finely diced
½ medium-sized white onion,
peeled and finely diced
Fresh cilantro, chopped
Juice of ¼ lime
½ teaspoon Kosher salt

FRESH TOMATO SALSA

Mix all the ingredients together; taste carefully and correct seasoning. Out-of-season tomatoes may need a pinch of sugar to bring up flavor.

Ahead-of-Time Note: See preceding avocado relish.

**INGREDIENTS FOR ABOUT
1-½ CUPS**

4 plum tomatoes, stemmed and
finely diced
¼ medium-sized white onion,
peeled and finely diced
1 serrano chile, stemmed,
seeded, and finely diced
Juice of ¼ lime
Fresh cilantro, chopped
½ teaspoon Kosher salt
Freshly ground black pepper
Pinch of sugar (if needed)

COOK'S NOTES

Nancy Silverton

La Brea Bakery & Campanile, Los Angeles

With its long hours and hot ovens, baking is not a cushy job, but it's the one that Nancy Silverton has enthusiastically chosen. "I wake up every day knowing I'm doing what I want."

When Nancy was studying for a liberal arts degree in California she needed a job and began working as a vegetarian cook in the dormitory kitchen. That changed her life. She knew immediately that cooking was what she really wanted to do, and after a year's apprenticeship, for free, she attended the London Cordon Bleu, which, in turn, gave her the confidence to apply to the then "in" restaurant, Michael's in Santa Monica. The only position open to her was in pastry—her least favorite. She took it anyway, thinking she would soon find another opening. Instead, she fell in love with baking and, to perfect her new craft, she attended the École Lenôtre near Paris. Studying with the master pâtissier was a turning point; shortly after returning home she worked with Wolfgang Puck at Ma Maison and later became his head pastry chef at Spago.

She met her husband, Chef Mark Peel, while he also was at Ma Maison. When they decided to open the restaurant, Campanile, they found a space big enough to accommodate both a restaurant and a bakery, and they began to build the ovens of what would be La Brea Bakery. "The problem was," said Nancy, "I had no idea how to bake bread! I kind of worked backward—I opened a bakery and then learned to bake." After another course with Lenôtre, she began her own experiments. "I lived bread twenty-four hours a day for six months."

Her bread is now considered one of the best and most innovative in the Los Angeles area, and she has been so generous as to give us one of the most important secrets of its popularity—her very special sourdough grape starter, along with her rustic loaf, focaccia, and her always popular olive loaf.

Bread Starter

One of the most important ingredients in bread making is the yeast that makes the dough rise. Many of Nancy Silverton's breads are made with a starter, or yeast batter, which gives a slow rise; and it is this slow rise that produces a beautiful brown crust plus an inside, or "crumb," with large holes and a pleasantly chewy texture. Her unique homemade starter uses grapes as a fermenting, yeast-producing agent and gives her breads their very special taste. Although you will need a good 10 days to produce it, there is nothing difficult in the process, and the starter will be yours forever since it can be kept alive indefinitely.

The Initial Starter Mixture—6 days: Stir the flour and water together in the container, mixing well—but do not worry about a few lumps, they will disintegrate later. Lay the grapes on a double layer of the washed cheesecloth and tie opposite corners together to form a bag. Lightly crush the grapes with a rolling pin, then swish the bag through the flour/water mixture and submerge. Cover tightly with a lid or with plastic wrap and a rubber band. Leave at room temperature for 6 days, stirring it up once a day.

The bag of grapes will gradually appear inflated, and liquid will begin to separate from the flour base. The mixture will begin to taste and smell slightly fruity, and the color will be strange. That is as it should be. By the sixth day, the bag of grapes will have deflated, the color will be yellow, and the taste pleasantly sour: the fermentation is complete. The starter is living but weak, and it needs to be fed.

Feeding the Starter—3 days: Lift out the bag of grapes and squeeze their juices back into the starter, then discard the grapes. Stir up the starter thoroughly, transfer it into a clean container. (Although you can use it after just one feeding, the starter will be stronger and healthier with the full treatment.) Three days before you plan to use it, stir 1 cup of flour and 1 cup of water into the container, blending well. Let stand uncovered at room temperature until it bubbles up—3 or 4 hours—then cover and refrigerate. Repeat the feeding the second day, and again on the third, and your starter is ready to use.

Storing the Starter: Store the starter tightly covered in the refrigerator, where it will keep perfectly for 4 to 6 months—

STARTER

2 cups bread flour, plus 3 more cups for later feedings (hard-wheat flour—look for it in a health food store if it is not in your market)

2-½ cups tepid (70° F) tap water, plus 3 more cups for later feedings

½ pound stemmed red grapes

SPECIAL EQUIPMENT SUGGESTED

A 2-quart glass or plastic container

1 yard washed and well-rinsed cheesecloth

Bread Starter (continued)

after which it is a good idea to pour off all but 2 cups and give it another feeding. Before using the stored starter for bread, however, give it the full 3-day feeding schedule once again to strengthen it and to tone down excess sourness. It is then ready to use.

Note: Always bring the starter to room temperature before using.

ALTERNATIVE STARTER: OVERNIGHT YEAST BATTER

As an alternative starter, the following overnight yeast batter produces a fine result, with a moist crumb but no special personality.

1 package fresh or dry-active yeast
¼ cup tap water (70° F) in a 1-cup measure
¼ teaspoon sugar
1 cup all-purpose flour
1 cup water, droplets more if needed

Crumble or sprinkle the yeast over the water in the measure, whisk in the sugar, and let rise for several minutes until it begins to foam. Whisk it again, then scrape into a 2-quart glass or plastic container. Whisk in the cup of flour, then the water, to make a mixture the consistency of pancake batter. Set uncovered at room temperature for several hours, until it foams and produces big heavy bubbles. Stir it up, and leave overnight. May be used in place of the Silverton starter in any of the following recipes.

Ahead-of-Time Note: If not to be used the next day, cover and refrigerate. The batter will gradually turn into a sourdough: feed it and treat it in the same way as the finished Silverton starter.

Rustic Bread Dough

This is the general formula for making Nancy Silverton's very special bread, with its sturdy brown crust, its moist and lightly chewy interior, and its real taste and real body. It is her special lightly sour starter and the slow risings she gives the dough that make her bread unique. Here is the formula not only for her country loaf but for such variations as herb bread, olive bread, walnut bread, as well as focaccia, bread sticks, rolls, and whatever other breadlike marvels your imagination brings forth.

Manufacturing Note: This is a heavy, moist dough, and is easiest to make in a food processor. However, if your machine is too small or not powerful enough for the following proportions, divide the ingredients in half and make the dough in two batches, then combine them for the final kneading by hand.

TIMING: 5 to 6 hours

Mixing the Dough: Measure the flour into the bowl of the processor, then add the starter. Measure out the rest of the ingredients and mix the milk and water together. Turn on the machine (to medium high, depending on your model) and keep it running while you add 1 cup of the water-milk mixture in a thin stream, then the olive oil, and finally the yeast. Process for 20 to 25 seconds, add the salt, and process 5 seconds more. Remove the lid to acquaint yourself with the dough. You should have a thick, fairly smooth batter, about the consistency of soft cooked oatmeal; process in more water by spoonfuls if too thick (the amount of water needed will depend on how thick your starter was). Taste it, adding more salt if needed.

A Short Rest: Let rest uncovered for 5 minutes. This allows the flour particles to soften and swell as they absorb the liquids.

Second Processing: Process again for 20 seconds (or more if dough is lumpy) to assure a smooth mix. Again, if the batter seems too thick, process in droplets of water.

First Rising of the Dough—2-½ hours or more at about 72° F: Lightly oil the rising bowl, then scrape the dough into it. Cover with plastic wrap and let rise to double its volume. The dough is now ready to use in the two following recipes.

Rustic Bread

Fat, puffy, and roughly rectangular, this easily formed and easy-to-serve informal loaf looks like a very thick focaccia. Its pleasantly distinctive, not too sour taste results from the recent feeding of its starter. Its crumb, with its lacy look and large holes, is due to its soft batter-type dough. Cut it into thick slices or break it into chunks and serve with soups, stews, salads, or cheese . . . take it on a picnic . . . stuff it for sandwiches . . . it makes wonderful toast.

INGREDIENTS FOR TWO 9-BY 12-INCH LOAVES, OR ONE LOAF AND SIX FOCACCIAS

7 cups (2 pounds) bread flour

2 cups starter (see preceding recipe or Alternative Starter in Box)

3 tablespoons milk

1 cup or more tepid water (70° F)

3 tablespoons olive oil, plus extra for oiling the bowl

1 package (1 tablespoon) dry yeast dissolved in 2 tablespoons water

1 tablespoon salt

SPECIAL EQUIPMENT SUGGESTED

A food processor with steel blade

A 6-quart mixing bowl (for rising the dough)

A 2- by 2-foot wooden, plastic, or marble work surface

Rustic Bread (continued)

INGREDIENTS FOR TWO
9- BY 12-INCH LOAVES,
ABOUT 2 INCHES THICK, OR
ONE LOAF AND SIX 6-INCH
ROUND FOCACCIAS

Rustic bread dough
1 cup or so each: flour and
either semolina flour or
finely ground white
cornmeal

SPECIAL EQUIPMENT
SUGGESTED

A 2- by 2-foot bread or cutting
board
2 dough scrapers
Parchment paper, about 2-½
feet
A pizza stone or ceramic
bread tiles, and a bread
peel (available from most
good cookware departments,
gourmet shops, and
catalogs)
A spray bottle for spritzing the
oven with water

Forming the Dough: Sprinkle the board quite liberally with some of the flour and some of the semolina or cornmeal, then pour the dough on it in as rectangular a shape as possible. It is important here during all of the forming not to stretch the dough any more than necessary, so as not to disturb its bubbly interior structure. Gently tuck and push the edges with your dough scraper to form a rectangle about 9 by 12 inches. Sprinkle the top of the dough lightly with flour, cover with a clean, dry cloth, and allow to rest for 20 minutes.

Dividing the Dough: Cut two pieces of parchment paper approximately 12 by 20 inches and sprinkle with flour and semolina. Using a dough scraper, gently divide the dough on the board into two equal pieces. Carefully scoop up one of the pieces, using a pair of dough scrapers, and arrange it on the floured paper, working the dough as little as possible but nonetheless pushing and prodding it into a rectangular shape about 9 by 12 inches. Repeat with the second piece of dough. Dimple the entire surface of one (which will be your bread loaf) at 3-inch intervals by pressing your floured fingers all the way down through the dough.

Letting the Dough Rise—2 hours: Sprinkle both rectangles with flour and cover with a clean, dry cloth. Allow to rise at room temperature for 1-½ to 2 hours or more until springy, soft, and alive; when you press the top of the dough lightly with two fingers, the pressure marks remain for a short time. Refrigerate the undimpled loaf, covered, which will be used for the focaccias (recipe follows); or for a second rustic loaf.

One Hour Before Estimated Baking Time: Place the baking stone or tiles on the oven rack in the lower third of the oven. Preheat the oven to 500° F for 25 minutes. Cut an additional piece of parchment paper and sprinkle quite liberally with flour and semolina.

Transferring the Dough to the Oven: Carefully lift the loaf on its parchment paper and, with one quick motion, invert it onto the new piece of floured paper. (If necessary, trim the paper so there is only a 1-inch border around the dough.) Spritz the oven liberally with water and close the door for 5 seconds to trap the steam. Slide the bread peel under the paper, then quickly open the oven door and slide the dough onto the hot baking surface, jerking away the peel. Immediately turn the oven temperature down to 450° F.

Baking the Bread—About 55 minutes: Spritz the oven with water every 3 minutes for 15 minutes. As soon as the bread is firm enough to move, slide the peel between the bottom crust and the paper and, lifting the bread, pull out the paper. Rotate the loaf to ensure even baking and bake until the top is golden brown—about 30 minutes. Turn the bread over to brown the bottom about 10 minutes longer.

When Is It Done? It sounds crisp and hollow when thumped. Remove to a rack and let cool for ½ hour or so before serving.

Note: Best eaten the day it is baked. Otherwise, cut the loaf in half crosswise and freeze in two separate packages.

Focaccia

Nancy Silverton's focaccias are like individual 6-inch pizzas except that they are puffy and made from her special rustic dough. Decorate the tops with pieces of caramelized onions, peppers, and cheese and eat like a pizza. Or use decorated focaccias for sandwiches, splitting them open and filling them with roasted vegetables, herbs, and goat cheese, for instance. Nancy says that even if you are a novice, you cannot go wrong with focaccias when you top and fill them in fragrant and appetizing ways.

Dividing the Dough: Stretch the dough very gently so you can cut it into six disks with a 5-inch dough cutter. Fold in half—reserve scraps for bread sticks (see end of recipe). Cover with a clean, dry cloth and let rest 15 minutes.

Forming the Dough: Press each of the folded disks again into a disk approximately 5 inches in diameter and place them 2 inches apart on the parchment-lined baking sheets. Brush the tops with olive oil.

The Toppings: Press the greens into the dough around the edges of the disks. Fill the centers with your choice from the suggestions listed—roasted peppers, new potatoes, pearl onions, and cheese, for instance—pressing the ingredients into the dough as you add them.

Final Rising: After filling, let the focaccias rise uncovered at room temperature for 1 hour. Meanwhile, preheat the oven to 500° F in time for

INGREDIENTS FOR 6 FOCACCIAS

½ Rustic Bread Dough recipe, page 84
½ cup or so each: flour and either semolina flour or finely ground white cornmeal
Olive oil
Bitter salad greens in smallish sprigs (such as frizzy lettuce, arugula, et cetera)

(continued)

Focaccia (continued)

Grated Parmesan cheese
Topping and/or filling
   suggestions: any vegetable
   that can be baked or
   roasted and still remain
   juicy and/or full of flavor
   (see suggestions at end of
   recipe).

baking, placing an oven rack on the top level—or on the top and upper-middle levels if you have two pans, in which case switch pans once or twice during baking.

Baking the Focaccias—30 minutes: When the oven is at 500° F, slide in the baking sheet (or sheets) and immediately turn the temperature down to 450° F. Spritz the oven with water 3 times at 5-minute intervals. Bake bread for 25 to 30 minutes or until golden brown. Remove from oven and place on a rack to cool.

TOPPING AND FILLING SUGGESTIONS

To Be Used As Is: cherry tomatoes; slivers or fingers of goat cheese, cheddar, Roquefort, et cetera; herbs, such as basil leaves, rosemary, sage; chunks of sausage or ham.

To Be Roasted: Group vegetables together on an oiled roasting pan according to their approximate cooking times. Brush with olive oil, then season lightly with salt, pepper, and such herbs as thyme, rosemary, or a mixture. Roast until each vegetable is tender. Suggested vegetables: quartered new potatoes, small white onions, and large peeled garlic cloves (30 minutes each), or fat slices of green, yellow, and/or red peppers (10 to 15 minutes), and so forth.

Caramelized Onions: Always useful, particularly as a simple sandwich topping. For example, cook 3 cups of sliced onions over low heat in a covered pan with 2 tablespoons of olive oil, ¼ teaspoon of salt, and a big pinch of sugar for 8 to 10 minutes or until tender and translucent. Uncover pan, raise heat to moderate, and let brown nicely—a droplet or two of wine vinegar added near the end gives a spritely touch.

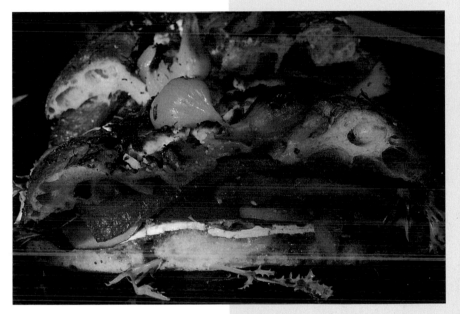

FUN WITH LEFTOVERS

Since you will have leftover dough from cutting out the focaccias, shape it into whatever you wish, following the general focaccia system. For example, make bread sticks by rolling out the equivalent of about 1 cup of dough with the palms of your floured hands on a well-floured board until you have an even, long roll 1 inch in diameter and 18 inches long. Arrange the rolls 1-½ inches apart on the lined baking sheets, then brush with olive oil. Garnish by spritzing tops with water, sprinkling with coarse salt, and tucking in sprigs of fresh rosemary every 3 inches along the length. Or spread a thin layer of caramelized onions over the tops and sprinkle with Parmesan cheese. Let rise for 1 hour. Slip them into a preheated 500° F oven and bake the same as the focaccias.

SPECIAL EQUIPMENT
SUGGESTED

2 pastry scrapers
A 5-inch round dough cutter
Parchment-lined baking sheets
A pastry brush
A spray bottle for spritzing the
oven with water

Olive Bread

Nancy Silverton's sturdy olive bread has the delicious aroma of real olives—but not overpoweringly so. This time the dough has the feel of a regular conventional dough but is made with her famous grape starter. Olive bread is one of her customers' favorites—how fortunate we can now make it in our own kitchens.

INGREDIENTS FOR TWO 8- TO 9-INCH ROUND LOAVES

7 cups bread flour, a little more if needed

2 teaspoons raw wheat germ

2 teaspoons fragrant dried thyme, coarsely ground

1-⅓ cups Nancy Silverton's starter, or the yeast-batter alternative, page 84

2 cups tap water, 70° F

1 tablespoon salt

1 cup each: Greek Kalamata olives and oil-cured olives, pitted and roughly chopped

1 package (1 tablespoon) active dry yeast (optional)

SPECIAL EQUIPMENT SUGGESTED

A food processor fitted with a steel blade (if your machine is too small for the proportions here, make the dough in two batches and combine them for the final hand-kneading)

A dough scraper

(continued)

Mixing the Dough and First Machine Kneading: Measure the flour, wheat germ, thyme, and starter into the bowl of the processor. Add the optional dissolved yeast *only* if your starter was not fully alive—bubbly throughout—after its final feeding. (If you are using the yeast-batter alternative, you will not need the additional yeast.) Start the machine and slowly pour in the water, then the salt. Process until the dough masses and balls up and rotates under the cover for 10 to 15 revolutions. Uncover the processor bowl and inspect the dough: it should be fairly smooth, soft, and a bit sticky when squeezed between thumb and finger. (If too wet and sticky, sprinkle in and process briefly a tablespoon or so of flour; if too stiff, process in droplets of water.)

Second Machine Kneading: Let the dough rest 5 to 10 minutes, allowing the flour particles to absorb the liquid. Process again for 15 to 20 revolutions, then uncover the machine.

Adding the Olives and Preparation for Hand-Kneading: Add the olives to the machine, and process into the dough with short on-off spurts. You just want to incorporate the olives, not chop them. Turn the dough onto a lightly floured board and knead by hand for several turns to be sure the olives are well incorporated, and that the dough is smooth. Divide in half with the scraper. Tuck all sides of each piece under itself and rotate the dough briefly with your palms to form a ball shape. Cover with a clean, dry cloth and let the dough rest on the board for 15 minutes.

Forming the Dough: One at a time, with the palms of your hands roll each ball of dough around, pulling the bottom against the board, creating tension to stretch the covering "skin" smoothly over the entire surface of the dough. If more tension is needed, spritz the surface of the dough with a little water. Cupping your hands around the ball and using pressure against the board, continue rotating until the ball is uniformly smooth, with no blisters or breaks. Turn the ball over, pinch the center of the bottom together to seal, and place pinched side down in a floured basket.

Letting the Dough Rise—2 hours: Leave the baskets uncovered at room temperature for 1-½ to 2 hours, or until the dough has started to rise. Enclose each basket in plastic wrap and refrigerate overnight.

Preparations for Baking: Take the baskets from the refrigerator and remove the wrapping. Let the dough warm almost to room temperature for 1-½ to 2 hours—it is important that it not be chilled.

Half an Hour Before Estimated Baking Time: Place the baking stone or tiles on the oven rack in the lower third of the oven and preheat to 500° F.

Slashing the Dough: Gently invert each basket, catching the dough in your hand and laying it carefully on a lightly floured wooden peel. With a single-edged razor, make a quick slanting ½-inch slash in the top of the dough from one side to the other. Open the slash slightly with your fingers.

Baking the Bread—45 minutes. Spritz the oven liberally with water and close the door for 5 seconds to trap the steam. Then quickly open the door and slide the dough onto the hot baking surface, jerking away the peel. Immediately turn down the oven temperature to 450° F. Continue spritzing the oven with water every 3 minutes for the first 15 minutes of baking. When the breads are firm enough, rotate their positions to ensure more even coloring. Continue baking for about 30 minutes. The cut should open up and the bread will rise to almost double its original size.

When Is It Done? The crust will be a deep golden brown, with visible small fermentation bubbles particularly around the base. When tapped on the bottom, the bread should make a hollow sound—the temperature on an instant thermometer plunged into the bottom of the loaf should be 200° F. Remove the bread to a rack to cool completely before slicing.

A 2- by 2-foot wooden, plastic, or marble work surface
Two wicker baskets about 10 inches across and 4 inches deep, lined with a clean, dry cloth and lightly floured
An instant meat thermometer
A bread peel
A pizza stone or ceramic bread tiles (you will find these in most good cookware departments, gourmet shops, and catalogs)

Jan Birnbaum

A determined fellow like Jan Birnbaum never does anything halfway— just catch a glimpse of him as he flies by on the biggest, fastest bike in the Harley-Davidson lineup. It's the bike he made up his mind to have just as he made up his mind to follow a five-and-a-half-year engineering education at the University of Louisiana with a culinary career—a field that had always appealed to him. He'd had a few restaurant jobs in college, but he certainly was not skilled enough to apply to important restaurants such as the famous K-Paul's Louisiana Kitchen. He applied anyway. Naturally Paul Prudhomme didn't hire him on the spot, but Jan relentlessly pestered the patient Prudhomme who finally said, "I see I'm not going to get rid of you so come to work."

K-Paul's was the start of a carefully charted and varied journeyman apprenticeship for Jan, who knew that he wanted a wide range of experience. His youthful days had given him rich and varied layers of influence—he grew up with Polish parents from Brooklyn in Baton Rouge, Louisiana, where he was surrounded by Italian neighbors whom he still refers to by familial names. "Grandma Valica" taught him to bake bread and he still loves the quiet, straightforward art of baking.

After four years with Chef Paul, he left "the-bottom-of-the-pot-flavors cooking" of K-Paul's and pursued an experience at the very opposite extreme—with Barry Wine at New York's Quilted Giraffe, where flavors were distinct and the presentation exacting. In spite of the great abyss that seemingly divides these two restaurants, Jan noted an important similarity in the two chefs. "They didn't accept the natural parameters of the kitchen and were willing to stretch them. Sometimes it ended in disaster, but more often it was responsible for some of their greatest successes."

Following his work at "The Giraffe," Jan spent a year at the Rattlesnake Club in Denver with Michael McCarty and Jimmy Schmidt, thus adding yet another dimension to his work. Before becoming Executive Chef at the Campton Place in San Francisco, he was sous-chef there under Bradley Ogden. Jan is pleased with the refinements his journeyman experiences have given to his New Orleans' base. The flavors of his dishes are sometimes intense, like the Louisiana sassafras crust on his leg of lamb; at other times they have the delicacy of his citrus dessert. And so often such dishes as one he presents to us here, his Scrambled Egg Torte, are simple in essence but stunningly original in presentation.

Home-Smoked Salmon

You can, of course, buy good smoked salmon, but if you want to smoke your own—and it's not at all difficult to do when you have a smoker—here is Jan Birnbaum's recipe.

Brining the Salmon: Measure the brine ingredients into the roasting pan and blend thoroughly. Lay the salmon in the pan, skin side down—the fish should be submerged—otherwise, plan to baste it several times during its marinade. Cover with plastic wrap and refrigerate for 1 hour. Remove the salmon from the liquid and dry thoroughly in paper towels—if damp, it will steam rather than smoke. Brush lightly with olive oil, place skin side down on a plate and strew the top with bruised herbs.

Smoking the Salmon: Fire up the smoker according to its directions, and when ready set the salmon, skin side down, on the top rack (farthest from the heat source). Cover the machine and smoke to the doneness you prefer—timing depends on the heat of the smoker. Chef Jan likes his

INGREDIENTS

Brine for the salmon
¼ medium Spanish onion, peeled and roughly chopped
½ cup Kosher salt
1 bay leaf, crushed
6 cloves garlic, smashed
¼ cup white vinegar
6 to 8 black peppercorns, crushed
2 cups water

(continued)

Home-Smoked Salmon (continued)

The salmon

18 to 24 ounces center-cut fresh salmon (skin on)

3 tablespoons olive oil

1 bunch chervil (about 25 sprigs), bruised with the back of a heavy knife (use parsley and a little more tarragon if you can't find chervil)

1 bunch fresh tarragon (about 20 sprigs), also bruised with knife, or 2 tablespoons fragrant dried tarragon

SPECIAL EQUIPMENT SUGGESTED

A stainless steel roasting pan just roomy enough to hold the fish and brine easily

A home smoker with fruit-wood chips (available in most hardware and sporting goods stores)

medium rare—press with your finger to test, and flake a piece to see and taste. Set on a bowl of ice cubes to cool briefly, then flake the barely warm salmon, gently pulling the flesh apart crosswise with your fingers to separate it into its natural flakes. Cover with plastic wrap and refrigerate.

Ahead-of-Time Note: The salmon may be prepared to this point up to 3 days in advance.

Smoked Salmon with Scrambled Egg Torte

Jan Birnbaum has ideas for eggs other than a plain breakfast. Here, for instance, although he does scramble them he also molds them into a cake-shaped torte that he then decorates with smoked salmon and tops with caviar and sour cream—and that takes scrambled eggs just about as far as they can go. Serve the torte for a fancy breakfast or brunch, or as the main course of a luncheon spectacular.

Preparing the Mold for the Eggs: Heavily butter the inside of the ring mold. Arrange slices of the bread in a 12-inch square and cut into a disk shape the size of the bottom of the mold. Fit the bread snuggly into the mold. Set the mold under a moderately hot broiler, watching carefully, until the side of the toast is lightly browned.

Preparing the Eggs: Shortly before you plan to serve, whisk the eggs in a mixing bowl to break up the yolks and to blend them thoroughly with the whites, and also to incorporate a little air. (Chef Jan adds no seasoning at this point.) Whisk in the cream. Preheat the oven to 300° F.

Scrambling the Eggs: It is important to cook the eggs very slowly, so they will remain a tender custard. Melt the butter over low heat in the frying pan. Pour in the eggs and stir constantly with the flat part of a rubber spatula. As the eggs finally begin to set, add 2 tablespoons of the finely cut chives, and salt and pepper to taste. When the eggs reach the consistency of applesauce, pour them over the toast in the mold and then smooth the top with the spatula. Set in the oven for 4 to 6 minutes, until the eggs have set just enough to be removed from the mold.

Serving the Torte: Run a sharp knife around the eggs to loosen them from the sides of the mold and transfer them on their false bottom to a warm serving platter. Rapidly encircle the sides of the torte with pieces of salmon, and arrange a loose mound of salmon in the center of the custard. Top with a spoonful of *crème fraîche* or sour cream and, if you have it on hand, spoon over an egg-shaped portion of caviar. Sprinkle with the finely chopped red onion or scallions and the remaining chives, and drizzle with cream. Stand a whole chive or two around the mounded salmon, then serve while still warm.

COOK'S NOTES

INGREDIENTS FOR 8 TO 10 SERVINGS

For the mold
1 loaf of egg or brioche bread (or white sandwich bread)

For the scrambled eggs
20 "large" eggs
1 cup half-and-half cream
1 tablespoon unsalted butter
4 tablespoons minced chives
1-½ teaspoons Kosher salt
1 teaspoon ground white pepper

For the topping
The preceding Home-Smoked Salmon or 1-¼–1-½ pounds store-bought smoked salmon
½ cup crème fraîche (or sour cream)
2 ounces best-quality caviar— Chef Jan prefers Osetra (optional)
1 small red onion or several scallions, minced
Several tablespoons heavy cream
2 to 3 whole chives

SPECIAL EQUIPMENT SUGGESTED

An 8-inch false-bottomed ring mold, or spring form pan 2-½ to 3 inches deep
A cookie sheet lined with parchment paper
A 10- to 12-inch, no-stick frying pan

Louisiana Sassafras Roasted Leg of Sonoma Lamb

It is a handsome sight on the dinner table: a whole leg of lamb roasted brown and beautiful under Jan Birnbaum's spicy crust from the land of the bayous. An additional feature is its long marinade in herbs, garlic, and olive oil, which both flavors and tenderizes the meat. To get any meaningful result from the marinade, however, you'll want to start proceedings 2 to 3 days before you plan to roast.

INGREDIENTS FOR 10 TO 12 SERVINGS

For the meat

9- to 10-pound whole, properly aged leg of lamb— hip and tail assembly removed, finely chopped, and reserved for stock (Chef Jan, of course, prefers that you choose to roast Sonoma lamb)

For the herb-and-garlic marinade

6 large whole heads of garlic, unpeeled, coarsely chopped

2 bunches thyme (40 sprigs), washed, dried, coarsely chopped

2-½ cups olive oil

For the lamb stock

The chopped bones and meaty scraps from the lamb, plus

(continued)

Marinating the Lamb—overnight or up to 3 days: Trim excess fat off the lamb, leaving a covering ⅛-inch thick. Score the fat-covering with cross-hatched knife-point cuts ¹⁄₁₆-inch deep, at 1-½-inch intervals.

Mix the marinade ingredients together in the roasting pan. Turn the leg of lamb in the pan to cover thoroughly, then scrape lamb and marinade into the plastic bag (do not wash the pan yet) and close the bag securely. Turn the lamb in the marinade bag twice a day, and leave at least overnight or up to 3 days.

Preparing the Lamb Stock and Lamb Sauce—About 1 hour of oven browning, then 2 to 3 hours of mostly unattended simmering: Spread the meat bones and scraps in the roasting pan, baste lightly with oil, and brown slowly in the middle level of a 400° F oven, stirring them up every 20 minutes or so. When lightly browned, stir in the coarsely chopped vegetables and continue until bones and vegetables are almost a mahogany brown but not burned.

Transfer the bones and vegetables to a stockpot; pour out and discard the fat in the pan. Deglaze the pan by pouring in a cup or so of water, setting it over heat, and scraping up coagulated roasting juices. Pour these into the stockpot along with enough water to cover the ingredients by 2 inches. Bring to a simmer, skimming off fat occasionally for 20 minutes or so or until it no longer continues to rise. Add the red wine and thyme, and cover the pot loosely—it must have a little air circulation. Continue simmering, skimming occasionally and adding a little water if needed, for 2 or 3 hours or until you feel and taste that you have gotten

their all out of the ingredients. Strain through a cheesecloth-lined sieve into a saucepan; degrease thoroughly. (See degreasing directions, page 136.)

The Sauce: Bring the degreased stock to a boil, then boil slowly uncovered until it has reduced by about half and is lightly thickened. Add the peppers, toasted cumin seeds, and balsamic vinegar; salt very lightly. Simmer another 20 to 30 minutes, strain, and carefully correct seasoning.

Ahead of Time Note: Both stock and sauce may be made in advance. When cold, cover and refrigerate for several days or freeze for a month or more.

Preparing the Lamb for Roasting: 2 hours before roasting, remove the lamb from its plastic bag, scrape off and reserve the marinade, and dry the meat thoroughly in paper towels. Spread the Louisiana spice over the fat side of the lamb and pat in firmly. Preheat the oven to 400° F.

Roasting the Lamb—1-¼ to 1-½ hours: Just before roasting, brush the lamb and its spice covering with reserved garlic oil, then set the lamb on the rack in the roasting pan. Roast until your instant meat thermometer reads 130° F, or medium rare. Let rest outside the oven for at least 20 minutes before carving—the thermometer reading will gradually rise to about 140° F.

PREPARING GARLIC OIL AND ROASTED GARLIC PUREE FROM MARINADE:

Strain the garlic marinade used for the lamb. Pour the oil into a screw-cap jar and refrigerate, where it should keep for several weeks (use it for sautés and special flavorings). Turn the garlic itself into a covered pan and roast in a 300° F oven for ½ hour or more, until very tender. Puree through a sieve or vegetable mill and use to flavor mashed potatoes, sauces, soups, et cetera.

any available equal amount of other fresh lamb, beef, or veal bones and scraps

2 to 3 tablespoons vegetable oil

The following vegetables, coarsely chopped: 2 large peeled carrots, 2 large peeled white onions, 3 large celery stalks

¾ cup red wine

6 sprigs fresh thyme

For the sauce

½ jalapeño pepper, seeded and minced

Big pinch chipolte chili

2 tablespoons toasted cumin seeds (see page 136)

¼ cup balsamic vinegar

Salt

For the Louisiana spice
The following mixed together:

¼ cup ground sassafras leaves (gumbo filé), or an additional cup toasted cumin seeds

¼ cup cumin seeds toasted golden brown in a dry pan and ground in a blender or spice mill

1-½ teaspoons cayenne pepper

4 tablespoons salt

1 tablespoon granulated sugar

2 teaspoons ground black pepper

(continued)

Louisiana Sassafras (continued)

*A roasting pan to fit both the
lamb and your oven*

*A plastic bag to hold the lamb
and marinade*

*A strainer lined with washed
cheesecloth for the sauce*

A carving board

A gravy boat

INGREDIENTS FOR TWO
9-INCH PIES

**For two 9- by 2-inch walnut
crusts**

1 cup walnuts

2-⅔ cups all-purpose flour

½ teaspoon salt

1 tablespoon sugar

*1 stick (8 ounces) unsalted
butter, chilled and cut into
½-inch dice*

*1 "large" egg whisked with 2
tablespoons iced water*

*2 to 3 tablespoons iced water
in a separate measure*

1 egg white

Pinch salt

(continued)

Finishing the Sauce: After the lamb has set for 10 minutes or so, remove it to a carving board or serving platter and spoon the fat (not the juices) out of the roasting pan. Pour in the sauce and set over heat, scraping into the sauce all the roasting juices. Taste very carefully for seasoning, then strain into a hot gravy boat.

Serving the Leg of Lamb: Carve the lamb at the table, or carve it in the kitchen and present it at the table. Spoon a helping of the sauce onto a hot plate, then arrange a slice or two of lamb partly covering it. Accompany, for instance, with Chef Jan's Potato Salsify Pie, which follows, and a garnish of watercress or fresh cilantro.

Potato Salsify Pie

When you want a starchy something to go with grilled or roasted meats, this unusual creation is particularly attractive. It can also serve as the main course for a luncheon or supper along with a nice green salad or a platter of fine ripe sliced tomatoes.

The Pie Dough: Pulse the walnuts in the food processor with a tablespoon of flour until the nuts are coarsely chopped. Spread on a small roasting pan and toast in a 350° F oven for 5 to 7 minutes, to brown lightly. Remove ½ cup and reserve for final decorations. When completely cool, scrape the remaining ½ cup into the bowl of the food processor. Add the rest of the flour, salt, sugar, and chilled butter. Pulse the butter into the flour, but only until the mixture looks like very coarse meal. Turn on the machine and at once process in the egg-water mixture, adding more driblets of the separate iced water until the dough masses; be careful here not to overmix—the dough should not ball up on the blade. Turn the dough out onto a lightly floured board, hand-knead briefly, cut in two, and wrap each piece in plastic wrap. Refrigerate for 2 hours.

Ahead-of-Time Note: May be left in the refrigerator for 2 days, or freeze.

Forming the Crust: Roll dough into 14-inch circles and line buttered molds. Refrigerate for 1 hour.

Preheat the oven to 350° F.

For the salsify filling
1 cup olive oil
12 large cloves of garlic, smashed
1 quart chicken stock, more if needed to cover ingredients
2 bay leaves
½ cup white wine vinegar
¼ cup Kosher salt
½ bunch thyme (10 sprigs)
2 teaspoons rosemary leaves, coarsely chopped
2 pounds peeled salsify (oyster plant, page 137; if not available, substitute more potatoes)

For the potato filling
4 cups heavy cream
1 cup lamb stock
2 teaspoons salt
1 teaspoon ground black pepper
¼ teaspoon minced garlic
1-½ pounds "boiling" potatoes, unpeeled and sliced ¼-inch thick

For serving
½ cup toasted ground walnuts reserved from first step
2 tablespoons finely chopped thyme

(continued)

Baking the Crust: Line the crusts with lightweight aluminum foil and fill with dried beans (to weigh them down during baking). Bake in the pre-heated oven for about 15 minutes or until set. Remove the foil and beans. Whisk the egg white with a pinch of salt until foamy and paint the shells with a light coating, then return to the oven for 5 minutes.

The Salsify Filling: Bring all of the salsify filling ingredients except for the salsify itself to a boil. Simmer for 10 minutes, then add the salsify and simmer until it begins to soften. Remove the pan from heat and allow the salsify to cool in the liquid. (Reserve leftover liquid for soups and another day.)

Ahead-of-Time Note: Cooked salsify may be stored up to 3 days.

The Potato Filling: Bring the cream, lamb stock, salt, pepper, and garlic to a boil in a large saucepan. Add the potatoes and simmer several min-utes until just tender—taste slices to be sure.

Ahead-of-Time Note: Filling may be cooked several hours ahead; set aside uncovered.

Salsify Pie (continued)

Assembling and Serving the Pie: Use a perforated spoon to transfer the potatoes from the cream to the walnut crusts. Spread the cooked salsify neatly over the potatoes, trimming it to fit if necessary. Pour enough of the potato-boiling cream over the vegetables to coat them nicely. Bake at 350° F for 10 to 15 minutes until bubbling hot. Toss the remaining walnuts and thyme together and strew them over the top.

Cut the pies warm and serve.

Citrus Gratin with Sourwood Honey

A sweetly refreshing selection of orange, grapefruit, and tangerine segments arranged all together, topped with a tender zabaglione sauce, then lightly browned under the broiler—this is certainly a delicious way to end any meal, especially an important one.

INGREDIENTS FOR 8
SERVINGS

For the fruits and citrus syrup
4 blood oranges
3 grapefruits
4 tangerines
*1 cup "Sourwood" honey
(Chef Jan's favorite) or your
own favorite*
1 lime

For the zabaglione topping
5 "large" egg yolks
1 pinch salt
The citrus syrup
Powdered sugar, to garnish

"Zesting" the Fruit, and Candying the Peel: This is for final decoration, and is an optional but pretty finish. Julienne the zests (the colored part of the peel) of 1 blood orange, 1 grapefruit, and 1 tangerine and candy them in sugar syrup (see page 135).

Citrus Syrup for the Zabaglione Topping: Juice 1 blood orange, 1 grapefruit, and 1 tangerine. Pour into a saucepan and boil down to reduce by half, then stir in the honey. Set over a larger bowl of cold water and let cool.

Preparing the Fruit: Peel the tangerines and drop them into a bowl of cold water to soften their pulpy skin covering. Meanwhile, shave the two ends off the grapefruit, oranges, and lime so that they will stand upright. Cut into thin slices with a sharp knife, cut off the peel and white pith to reveal the flesh beneath. Separate the tangerines into segments and scrape their skins clear of pulp. Place the prepared slices in individual shallow bowls.

The Zabaglione Topping: Pour 2 inches of water in the pan of the chef's double boiler and bring to a simmer. Blend the egg yolks, salt, and citrus

(continued)

syrup together with the whisk in the stainless steel bowl. Set over the pan of simmering water, and whisk slowly with an up-and-down circular motion, beating air into the mixture as it slowly warms through. In about 5 minutes, with a nice broad whip, you should have a fine fluffy cream 5 to 7 times its original volume.

Ahead-of-Time Note: May be completed ½ hour or so in advance; keep slightly warm and beat up now and then.

Serving the Citrus Gratin: Preheat the broiler. About 5 minutes before serving, top the fruit-filled bowls with the zabaglione and place a few inches under the hot broiler, watching carefully until golden brown. Scatter the candied zests over the surface and top with a sprinkling of powdered sugar. Serve immediately.

CUOK'S NOTES

SPECIAL EQUIPMENT
SUGGESTED

A vegetable peeler
The chef's double boiler: an 8-inch saucepan topped with a tight-fitting stainless steel bowl
A large whisk
For serving: shallow ovenproof bowls

Jean-Louis Palladin

Chef Jean-Louis bringing home the ducks from the Hudson Valley Foie Gras duck farm.

Jean-Louis Palladin began to cook because he didn't want to go to school. At the age of twelve, he peeled vegetables at Le Franco Italien, a small restaurant near his hometown in the southwest of France. He had no aspirations at that time to be a chef; he just liked the restaurant kitchen better than the classroom. "I liked it. I liked it. I liked it. And then one day I loved it and made it my life." He enrolled in the hotel school in Toulouse to expand the classical training he had received as an apprentice. Before long, he was the saucier at the famed Hôtel de Paris in Monte Carlo, and soon after he moved to the world-renowned Plaza-Athénée in the heart of Paris. When, back in his hometown at the age of twenty-eight, he was awarded two Michelin stars for his restaurant, La Table des Cordeliers, he was the youngest chef in France ever to be so honored. Chef Jean-Louis was ecstatic, and he considered himself very lucky that his mentor, Rene Santrini, "was a man of taste who emphasized hard work and the classics."

After thirty-three years in the kitchen, Chef Jean-Louis still loves it—but then, this open and exuberant man has a good deal of passion for everything he does. "Life is fun. I don't take life too seriously. I want to do it right, but I was lucky to have the right beginnings to do that." The right beginnings were a mother from Spain and a father from Italy and a childhood in the southwest of France. He grew up with the tastes of three different countries and developed an early and long-lasting appreciation for their culinary traditions. "It's important to cook from your roots. I always keep traditional foods on my menu, but it's also necessary to be contemporary."

Jean-Louis Palladin has the reputation of a chef who is amazingly comfortable doing just that—blending contemporary and traditional ideas. He has been in Washington, D.C., since 1979, at Jean-Louis at the Watergate Hotel, where his hand-lettered menus change daily. Offering a variety was his greatest challenge when he first arrived in the United States, and he asked himself more than once why he had come. Today, he finds this country to be one of the best food places in the world and he feels that the influence of French chefs "helped trace a little path from their kitchens to ours." The path we are tracing here is to the southwest of France because Chef Jean-Louis has prepared a typical Gascon menu with top-notch quality American foie gras, meaty Hudson Valley duck breasts, and French Armagnac.

Fireplace-Roasted Duck Breast with Sautéed Porcini Mushrooms

Jean-Louis Palladin loves cooking in a fireplace; it reminds him of his childhood home in Gascony where the fireplace was almost as wide as the wall, always with a big pot of soup suspended over glowing embers. His new restaurant in Atlanta, Resto des Amis, has a twelve-foot fireplace, and he easily converts any home hearth for cooking, as he has done for these succulent herb-coated duck breasts.

Cooking in the fireplace is wonderfully simple and elemental, and if you wish to do so yourself, Chef Jean-Louis's directions are on page 104. You will enjoy it not only for duck breasts but for chicken, roasts, and even fish.

A Note on Duck Breasts and Wild Mushrooms: The duck breasts for this recipe are large; they come from Hudson Valley moulards, the kind that produce foie gras. Fortunately, many wild mushrooms are now available in our supermarkets, and if you can't find porcinis, pick something else for the quick sauté of garlic and woodsy mushrooms to accompany the duck.

Preparing the Duck Breasts for Roasting:

Trimming and Seasoning. Trim the duck breasts, cutting off extra fat around the edges. Remove the fillets (short strips of meat on underside, the flesh side) and save for another meal. With a sharp knife, score the fat side of the breast (not the meat) with crosshatches 1 inch apart. Sprinkle all over with the thyme leaves, a good amount of salt, and the pepper (the

INGREDIENTS FOR 4 TO 6 SERVINGS

For the duck breasts
2 or 3 boneless duck breast halves ("magrets"), about 1 pound each (see note, p. 107
6 sprigs fresh thyme, leaves removed from stems
Sea salt
Freshly ground black pepper
Duck fat or vegetable oil (Chef Jean Louis uses grapeseed oil)

(continued)

Duck Breast (continued)

For the mushrooms

*¾ pound porcini mushrooms,
or other wild mushrooms*

*¾ tablespoon foie gras fat or
vegetable oil*

Several whole garlic cloves

4 or 6 sprigs fresh thyme

Salt

Freshly ground black pepper

**SPECIAL EQUIPMENT
SUGGESTED**

White butcher's twine

*Glowing hardwood embers in
the fireplace, in time for
roasting (see box below)*

*A roasting pan to catch fat
and juices in the fireplace*

*A 10- to 12-inch no-stick,
sauté pan*

breasts should be well seasoned, since dripping duck fat will wash off much of it when they hang in the fireplace).

Tying. Cut a piece of twine about 5 feet long and dip it in duck fat or oil to prevent it from burning. Leaving a 2-foot piece free for hanging, loop the rest around the length of the breast and then tightly around the circumference to make a neat package of uniform thickness.

Roasting the Duck Breasts—30 to 40 minutes to medium rare: When the fire is ready for roasting, rub the breasts with duck fat or oil, tie the string to the tubing in the fireplace, and place the roasting pan under the breasts. The breasts will twist around by themselves but will need help from you now and then. Baste occasionally with accumulated fat in the roasting pan. The breasts are done to medium rare when they are just beginning to take on a springiness to the touch in contrast to their squashy raw state—130° F on an instant meat thermometer (which will gradually rise to about 140° F).

CONVERTING YOUR FIREPLACE

Using your fireplace to cook will involve a trip to a plumbing supply store, but the process is very easy. You will need a piece of copper or metal tubing, ½-inch thick, cut to the exact size of the horizontal opening at a spot about three feet above the hearth. Wedge the metal pipe into the opening, close to the front, so that it is firmly in place; this will be used to suspend the meat.

A piece of cast iron placed against the back wall of the fireplace, a back plate or fire plate is absolutely essential to reflect the heat and distribute it evenly. Chef Jean-Louis found his in an antique store, and if you live in an old house there may be one in place already.

Build the fire with hardwood, such as oak or hard maple, which will burn hot and long and keep the heat at a steady temperature. Suspend the meat so that it hangs about ½ foot above the hearth and a little more than that in front of the fire. Put a roasting pan under the hanging meat to catch the drippings.

Preparing the Mushrooms: While the duck breasts are roasting, trim the mushrooms, brush clean, and slice the stems and caps into ¾-inch pieces. Heat the reserved foie gras fat or oil in the sauté pan. Add the mushrooms and sauté to brown lightly, then add the garlic, thyme sprigs, salt, and pepper and sauté over moderate heat, tossing now and then, for 20 to 25 minutes. Remove the sprigs of thyme; taste, and correct seasoning.

Serving: Remove the twine from the duck breasts and cut into ½-inch crosswise slices. Spoon the sautéed mushrooms onto hot plates and arrange slices of duck over them, pouring the exuded juices over the meat. Serve at once.

COOK'S NOTES

Foie Gras with Poached Apples

It is certainly a great boon that fresh American foie gras is now available to us. You may have to special order it in your market, but it is worth every effort to track down. The flavor of foie gras is so rich and distinctive that it seldom needs much else. Chef Jean-Louis's recipe with apples has just a few ingredients, but the tart sweetness of the fruit with the full, deep flavor of the meat makes an absolutely delicious dish.

INGREDIENTS FOR 6 SERVINGS

For the apples
4 tart green apples (Granny Smith)
1 lemon, cut in half
1-½ cups sugar

For the foie gras
A whole 1-½- to 2-pound fresh duck foie gras*
Salt
Freshly ground black pepper
¼ cup sliced shallots (5 or 6 large shallots)
¼ cup dry port wine
1-¼ cups rich meat stock, preferably a homemade, gelatinous, well-reduced veal stock

SPECIAL EQUIPMENT NEEDED

A wide, 3-quart saucepan
A high-sided, 12-inch, no-stick sauté pan
A fine-meshed sieve, or chinois
A 2-ounce ladle

Preparing the Apple Garnish: Peel the apples and reserve the peel. Rub the apples with the half lemon to prevent discoloration, then halve and core them. Pour 3 cups of water into the 3-quart saucepan, add the apples, apple peels, the juice of half the lemon, the squeezed lemon itself, and sugar. Set over high heat and bring to the boil. Reduce the heat to low and let poach very slowly for 20 minutes, or until the apples are tender but not mushy. Remove the pan from heat and let the apples set in the syrup.

Preparing the Foie Gras: Beige-pink fresh foie gras consists of two long lobes attached at the large ends. Pull them gently apart with your hands and look them over carefully, especially in the area where they were attached. Pull out and discard any little tubes and veins, and if there are any darkish or greenish areas, shave them off—they are bitter because that's where the bile ducts lay. Season with salt and pepper.

Sautéing the Foie Gras—15 minutes: Lay the foie gras in the sauté pan; it needs no fat because it renders its own. Cook on high heat for 5 minutes, or until slightly browned. Gently turn with a rubber spatula and lower the heat. Add the shallots to the pan and cook 5 more minutes. Turn the foie gras again and cook another 5 minutes.

When Is It Done? When you press it with your finger, the liver has just become lightly springy in contrast to its squashy raw state—foie gras is served medium rare. Remove the smaller piece to a clean, dry cloth towel to drain. The larger piece will need a few minutes more; when done, remove it to the towel. Cover the foie gras with a second towel and set aside to keep warm.

Making the Sauce: Strain the fat from the sauté pan; retain the shallots, and return them to the pan. Pour in the port wine and about ¾ cup of apple cooking syrup. Scraping the coagulated juices into the liquid with a wooden spoon, boil down until it is almost syrupy. Add the meat stock and boil down again to a syrup. Pour the sauce through a fine-meshed sieve and press hard with the ladle to extract all juices from the shallots and apples. Return the sauce to the pan, and if it is too thick, stir in a little of the apple syrup. Blot the accumulated fat off the foie gras with paper towels and return to the sauce just to reheat.

Serving: For individual servings, dip out a poached apple, drain cut side down on a clean, dry towel, and place off center on a warm dinner plate. Slice the foie gras into ½-inch pieces and place several slices next to the apple on the plate. Spoon some of the sauce over the apple and foie gras and serve immediately.

Sources for foie gras, duck breast, and so forth: If your local gourmet emporium cannot supply these luxury items, here, as of this writing, are three reliable sources:

D'Artagnan	*Hudson Valley Foie Gras*	*Wine Country Foie Gras*
399-419 St. Paul Ave	*and Duck Products*	Guillermo Gonzalez & Assoc.
Jersey City, NJ 07306	A. G. Y. Corp.	P.O. Box 2007
	RR #1, Box 69	Sonoma CA 95476
	Ferndale NY 12734	

Prune Croustade with Armagnac Sauce

Chef Jean-Louis's prune croustade is a fine use for phyllo dough, which produces a delicious croustade for prunes and Armagnac. The multiple layers of paper-thin dough brushed with melted butter and coated with sugar bake to form a crisp package around the brandy-marinated fruit. Steeping the prunes overnight plumps them and permeates them with the earthy flavor of the Armagnac. Baked in a large rectangle with scrunches of golden-brown phyllo on top, this is a spectacular dessert that belies its essential simplicity.

INGREDIENTS FOR 12 SERVINGS

3-¾ pounds pitted prunes
2 cups sugar
2 cups water
1 cup Armagnac
3-½ sticks (14 ounces) unsalted butter, melted
1 package (16 ounces) phyllo dough, or 30 sheets top-quality frozen phyllo dough thawed according to package instructions, opened onto a tray and covered with a damp towel
Confectioners' sugar

Preparing the Prunes and the Sauce: Turn the prunes into a 3-quart mixing bowl, and measure in 1-½ cups of sugar, the water, and Armagnac. Stir briefly to dissolve the sugar, then cover the bowl with plastic wrap and refrigerate overnight. Drain the prunes when you are ready to use them, roughly slice them, and set aside in a bowl. Slowly boil down the juices by half, until lightly syrupy, and reserve; this is the sauce.

Preparing the Croustade:

Preliminaries. Preheat the oven to 400° F, and set the rack in the upper third level. Cut a piece of parchment paper to fit the bottom of the pastry pan exactly. Paint the parchment paper and the sides of the pastry pan lightly with melted butter. Cut 18 layers of phyllo dough the same size as the paper, and cover with a clean, damp towel—it is essential that the dough remain soft and pliable.

Building the Phyllo Layers. Lay a sheet of dough over the parchment paper, brush the dough with 2 tablespoons of butter, and sprinkle evenly with a scant tablespoon of sugar. Lay a second sheet of dough over the first, paint with butter and sprinkle with sugar as before. Repeat with a third layer, then bake for about 5 minutes in the preheated 400° F oven, until nicely browned. Remove from the oven, brush with butter and lay a sheet of phyllo dough over the browned top; paint with butter and sprinkle with sugar as before. Add two more buttered and sugared layers of dough, bake again until brown. Finish with three more layers of buttered and sugared dough, browned again in the oven, making 9 layers in all.

Assembling the Croustade: Reduce the oven heat to 350° F. Spread the prunes evenly over the phyllo crust, bringing them to the very edge of the pan. Next, assemble the 9-layer top crust on top of the prunes in exactly the same manner as the bottom crust—baking each time after you have assembled the 3 buttered-sugared layers. When the last layers have browned, turn the thermostat up to 400° F.

Forming the Top: Scrunch up 12 pieces of uncooked phyllo dough to make rough rocky shapes. Arrange them over the top of the croustade, sprinkle with dribbles of butter and sugar, and brown in the oven for several minutes (if by chance the top refuses to brown, set 5 inches under a hot broiler for a few seconds, watching carefully).

Finishing the Dessert: Let cool 15 to 20 minutes, then dribble several spoonfuls of sauce over all and dust with confectioners' sugar.

Serving: Transfer the croustade to a serving platter, and present this quite wildly dramatic spectacle to your guests. Cut into portions with a sharp knife. As you do so, the top crust will crumble. Serve on dessert plates with one or two spoonfuls of the sauce dribbled around it.

Ahead-of-Time Note: The croustade can be made several hours and even a day or two ahead, but a freshly baked dessert is always most desirable.

SPECIAL EQUIPMENT
SUGGESTED

Parchment paper
A pastry pan, either a 10-½-
by 15-inch sheet pan or a
jelly-roll pan (which is a
little smaller, for smaller
ovens)
A pastry brush
A small-meshed sieve, for
powdered sugar
A long, very sharp knife

Alice Waters

Chez Panisse, Berkeley

Alice Waters started a revolution in August 1971, but like the woman herself it was a gentle, quiet uprising. When she opened Chez Panisse, she had already made a personal commitment to serve only the highest-quality products according to the season—no cardboard February tomatoes or tasteless winter strawberries. But eating according to the season is desirable only if the season is productive, and in the pre-Panisse days such things as arugula and frisé were merely foreign words, while blood oranges and Meyer lemons lived elsewhere.

Over the last two decades, Chef Alice Waters has foraged enthusiastically and encouraged a network of farmers, ranchers, and fishermen to provide her with the best possible ingredients. Her philosophy was simple: If there's a demand, then the farmers will plant it. If we ask often enough, we'll get it. Alice's quiet revolution has forever changed a generation of knowing cooks and consumers.

It's apropos that Alice should teach a nation to eat the freshest and best, since teaching had been her life's goal. She graduated from the University of California at Berkeley in 1967 with a degree in French Cultural Studies and then went to London to train at the famous and innovative Montessori School. When she finished her studies there, she went to France for a visit and immediately fell in love with it—so much so that she stayed a considerably longer time than she had planned. When she finally returned to Berkeley, she enthusiastically began to cook French dinners at her home for friends. When friends began to invite friends, the dinners grew so large she had to charge—thus was born Chez Panisse and its five-course, *prix-fixe* menu.

Alice Waters's modest beginnings have blossomed to include not only an upstairs, but also a stand-up café serving breakfast and lunch and named for her daughter, Fanny, who just happens to have her own cookbook, *Fanny at Chez Panisse*. There are four other Chez Panisse cookbooks, and a host of well-known chefs who began their careers with Chef Alice and carry on her tradition at their own restaurants.

Before Alice begins to cook, she grabs a big basket, heads off to the farmers' market, and, as she says, "let the vegetables lead me around." On the day we visited her, she had found tender baby beets and fennel bulbs, as well as a host of greens.

Prosciutto with Warm Wilted Greens

Most people think of winter as a dead time in terms of colorful vegetables, but Alice Waters sees the bounty of winter in their many shades of green. During those slow garden months, she garnishes every plate in the restaurant with a sauté of these tasty treasures that are so often discarded. The same technique and dressing can be used for a single green, but a variety is more interesting, since the distinct flavors come together to form a very special taste.

INGREDIENTS FOR 6 SERVINGS

For the greens
3 large handfuls of just-picked winter greens, washed and dried (such as a combination of mustard greens, kale, broccoli raab, spinach, turnip or beets tops, chard)
2 tablespoons olive oil
A large pinch of salt

For the vinaigrette
1 large garlic clove
¼ teaspoon salt

Preparing the Greens: Strip the leaves from their center stalks. Discard the stalks and coarsely chop the leaves into large pieces. If using a variety, mix them together. Pour the oil into the sauté pan and add just enough greens to fill the pan—the rest will go in once the first batch wilts. Pour a little water over the greens, cover the pan, and turn the heat to moderate. When this first batch has shrunk down—1 or 2 minutes—add the rest of the greens and a good pinch of salt. Cover the pan again and cook for 10 to 15 minutes, or until greens are wilted and tender. Check them as they cook, tossing occasionally with the tongs, and adding more water if the pan becomes dry. Let cool briefly, then squeeze the greens quite dry with your hands. Spread out on the platter and set aside.

Preparing the Vinaigrette: Peel the garlic, cut it into large pieces, and place in the mortar. Mash to a paste with the pestle, sprinkling in a little salt as you pound to bring out the juices and help soften the garlic.

(continued)

Prosciutto with Greens (continued)

2 tablespoons red wine vinegar
4 tablespoons excellent extra
    virgin olive oil
Freshly ground black pepper

For the garnish
12 very thin slices prosciutto
Mustard blossoms
    (if available)

**SPECIAL EQUIPMENT
SUGGESTED**

A large sauté pan with lid
A mortar and pestle (optional)
Tongs
A large serving platter

Occasionally scrape any small pieces of garlic clinging to the bottom of the pestle back into the mortar. When the garlic is an absolute paste, mash in the vinegar with the pestle and beat in the oil with a fork. Taste and add salt and pepper, if needed.

Serving: With your tongs, toss the greens in a bowl with enough vinaigrette to coat evenly. Form into a loose mound on the platter and arrange slices of prosciutto around the circumference. Garnish with mustard blossoms if you have them. Serve warm or cold.

CHOOSING AND USING GARLIC AND SHALLOTS

Anyone who loves as much garlic as Alice Waters should have a private reserve—and she has one—growing in great quantities around the house. When she wants a bulb, she opens her door, grabs one, and then also has the leaves to use in salads or to chop for garnish.

Since the characteristics of garlic change according to the seasons and where it is grown, Alice always pays attention to how much she uses and how she handles it. In July, for example, California garlic is irresistibly sweet, but in winter it can be very strong. Winter garlic often has a green sprout in the center, which is the bitter germ beginning to grow. She removes it if the garlic is to be used raw; it won't be noticed if the garlic is cooked.

The flavors of both garlic and shallots, once they are chopped, are extremely fickle and will oxidize and change quickly; chop only when needed, Alice advises, and add immediately to your other ingredients. Submerging them in an acid like vinegar or lemon juice will also prevent the oxidation. Chef Alice dices by hand garlic and shallots that are to be used raw because she feels crushing releases too many strong juices. When she wants the strong flavor of pureed garlic, she uses either a mortar and pestle (see page 111) or this ingenious fork-tine system. Hold a kitchen fork firmly on the counter with its tines facing down. Rub the cut half of a peeled garlic clove back and forth across the tines, and it will fall from the fork in a puree. Sprinkle on a little salt, and mash for a few seconds with the fork, until the garlic is a fine paste.

To remove the tenacious scent of garlic from your hands, wet them in cold water, rub with salt, and then wash in soap and warm water. Repeat if necessary using lemon juice, too, if you wish.

Green Olive Tapénade on Croutons

The pithy, piquant flavors of the Mediterranean come together in this recipe from Provence. *Tapénade* is an olive relish, and this one is made with green olives—the almond-shaped French *picholine*—but it can be made with any olive, black or green, that has a good strong essential taste and is not too salty.

Alice hand-chops her ingredients rather than pureeing them in a machine, since she prefers a certain look, texture, and taste—and hand chopping does indeed make a distinct difference. A well-made *tapénade* is a matter of balance, and no single flavor should dominate. Therefore, since the intensity of the ingredients is so variable consider that a *tapénade* is made by taste, and the amounts specified here are a guide only—you will add or subtract according to your own judgment.

A Note on the Capers and Anchovies: You may certainly use bottled capers and freshly opened canned anchovies rather than the salt-packed ones specified here, but in Alice's opinion the salt pack gives the better flavor. To find them, scout out real Italian groceries; there you can often

Tapénade (continued)

buy salted anchovies and capers one by one or in bulk. As long as you keep them covered with coarse Kosher salt, they will last for months in a covered jar under refrigeration.

INGREDIENTS FOR ABOUT 2 CUPS

For the tapénade

4 dozen green olives (picholine)
2 salt-packed anchovies
2 to 3 tablespoons salt-packed capers
1 small garlic clove
1-⅓ cups olive oil
1 lemon, cut in half
2 teaspoons cognac

For serving

4 pieces crusty country bread (6 by 4 inches by ½-inch thick)

SPECIAL EQUIPMENT SUGGESTED

A large knife
Tongs

Preparing the Tapénade:

The Olives. To remove pits, place an olive on your cutting board and hold the flat side of your knife on top of it; press down firmly, using the other hand to give a deliberate push. The olive will split and its pit is easily picked out. When all the pits have been removed, chop the olives finely and place in a bowl.

The Anchovies. Rub the excess salt from anchovies and rinse in cold water. Carefully pull each anchovy apart into its two fillets; pick out the small bone structure. Rinse and taste. If they are very salty, let soak in a bowl of cold water for 5 to 10 minutes. Pat them dry, finely chop, and add to the olives. (If you have taken them from a can of salted anchovies, spread a thin layer of Kosher salt over the unused ones, cover, and refrigerate.)

The Capers. Soak capers briefly in cold water to remove excess salt; drain, rinse in cold water, and pat dry. Finely chop and taste. If quite salty, stir by degrees into the olives and anchovies, adding only as much as you feel needed.

The Garlic. Peel garlic and hand-chop very fine. Add to the bowl, stir, and taste.

The Finish. Stir the olive oil into the chopped ingredients, then a good squeeze of lemon juice and the cognac. Stir and taste carefully, adding whatever you think it needs to make an interesting balance of flavors. Let the *tapénade* sit for 1 hour or so, allowing the flavors to blend.

Serving: Watching carefully, place the bread on a rack over an open fire (or under a broiler), turning once or twice, until toasty brown on each side. Spread the *tapénade* on the hot toast, cut into quarters, and serve at once.

THE BOUNTY OF WINTER

Chez Panisse has a "forager" whose job it is to seek out seasonal produce, such as the tenderest of winter greens and the freshest wild mushrooms. Since new winter varieties are cropping up all the time, winter's bounty can have the same colorful appeal as summer's. The selection that Alice Waters uses in her recipes may not yet be available where you live—but keep on asking.

Fennel: The heads of young Florence fennel are small and tender with delicate, feathery leaves. Older, larger heads have a good flavor and texture but a tough core that should be removed. Use the tops of the stalks to stuff fish and chop the leaves to sprinkle on finished dishes.

Beets: Red ones are the most common, but beets are available in other varieties—golden, maroon, pink. Look in farmers' markets and good greengrocers for young small beets. Boiling leeches out too much of the good beet taste, but steaming and Chef Alice's oven method on page 116 retain it. You can also use the pressure cooker. By the way, the tops of fresh young beets are tender enough to cook (see page 111).

Mushrooms: Fresh mushrooms are tightly closed and have a fresh clean smell. In older ones, the gills are exposed and the smell can be ammoniated—reject them. New varieties of wild mushrooms are appearing on the shelves all the time, as are the familiar wild varieties of cèpe or boletus and chanterelle.

Meyer Lemons: Now being grown in California, this lovely citrus fruit is larger and sweeter than the more common Eureka lemon. The thin-skinned Meyer has a delicate perfume and a sweet flavor that make it especially appealing for tarts and marmalades.

Blood Oranges: Many of us can recall the shocking first drink of this incredibly red fruit, thinking it was tomato. Abundant in the Mediterranean, quantities of sweet blood oranges are now being grown in California and to some extent in Florida. From the outside, they usually look like any other orange, but once cut they reveal a flesh that varies from a striated light red to an intense scarlet.

Beet, Blood Orange, Walnut, and Rocket Salad

It's a shame that beets are so often neglected, because they are a hearty, delicious, and versatile winter vegetable. Those who shun them may well be remembering the tinny taste of canned beets, which bears no resemblance whatsoever to the lovely flavor of the fresh beet. Then, of course, there's the predicament of red hands. Alice Waters solves it easily by rubbing her pink-tinged fingers in salt, then washing them in warm water. Those obstacles aside, there's every reason to try her citrus-dressed beet and blood orange salad on a bed of nutty arugula. If you're lucky enough to find a variety of different beets, by all means mix them together on the salad—cooking and dressing each separately so their colors won't bleed into each other. Alice, thanks to her almost daily pilgrimage to the farmers' markets, finds baby beets no more than 1 inch in diameter. But larger beets, although not as appealing, will make a beautiful salad, too.

INGREDIENTS FOR 6 SERVINGS

For the beets
2-½ pounds fresh beets
1 cup water
Salt
Freshly ground pepper

For the vinaigrette dressing
3 blood oranges (or regular oranges, though lacking the drama of the former)
1 large shallot
Salt
¼ cup sherry wine vinegar
½ cup excellent extra virgin olive oil

(continued)

Preparing the Beets—1 hour: Preheat the oven to 375° F. Wash the beets and cut away the tops and tails. Place in the baking dish, pour in water, and cover tightly with aluminum foil. Bake for 45 minutes to 1 hour (or longer), until the beets are tender enough to be pierced easily with a toothpick or a small knife. Remove foil, let the beets cool, and then peel them over the sink (their skins will rub off easily). Slice the beets thin; season with salt and pepper.

Preparing the Oranges:

The Orange-Sauce Base. Grate the zest (orange part of peel) of 1 orange into a small bowl, being careful not to include any white pith. Cut the orange in half and squeeze the juice from one half into the grated zest (set the second half aside in case you need it later).

The Orange Slices. From both ends of the 2 remaining oranges, cut slices deep enough to expose the flesh. Stand each orange on end and neatly slice off strips of skin and pith, from top to bottom, all around, to expose the naked flesh. Cut oranges into thin slices and set aside for the salad.

The Vinaigrette. Peel the shallot, cut into fine dice, and stir at once into the orange juice and zest. Add salt. Whisk the vinegar and then the oil into the bowl. Taste carefully and determine if more oil or vinegar is needed, or juice from the reserved orange half. The sauce should be on the acidic side, to balance the sweetness of the oranges and beets.

Serving: Arrange the rocket on the platter. Spoon a few tablespoons of vinaigrette over the beets, toss to coat evenly, and then place artfully on the rocket. Lay orange slices around the platter and scatter walnuts over the top. Spoon on enough vinaigrette to coat the salad. Serve immediately.

For serving

2 bunches rocket (arugula), washed and dried

½ cup walnut halves (toasted at 325° F for 8 to 10 minutes)

SPECIAL EQUIPMENT SUGGESTED

An 8- by 10-inch baking dish
A small-holed grater
A juicer
A serving platter

Shaved Fennel, Mushroom, and Parmesan Salad

The best ingredients are the best start for any recipe, but when a dish is as simple and quick to make as this salad they are crucial. Find a top-quality greengrocer or farmers' market and choose tender, fresh fennel bulbs and fragrant, tightly closed mushrooms. For wonderful fullness of taste, use real imported Parmesan cheese—*parmigiano reggiano.* The vegetables for this first-course salad are shaved absolutely paper-thin. (Alice, by the way, uses one of the small inexpensive vegetable slicers described on page 138.) Properly sliced, the vegetables and cheese release their perfumes while softening, so that they practically melt together.

INGREDIENTS FOR 4 SERVINGS AS A SMALL APPETIZER

2 small (or 1 large but tender)
* very fresh fennel bulbs*
Salt
Freshly ground pepper
3 to 4 tablespoons excellent
* extra virgin olive oil*
3 ounces (about 3 medium)
* cultivated mushrooms or a*
* fine, fresh 3-ounce* **Boletus**
* **edulis** (cèpe), brushed clean*
½ lemon
A big chunk of imported
* Parmesan cheese at room*
* temperature*

SPECIAL EQUIPMENT SUGGESTED

A vegetable slicer
A large serving platter
A hand-held cheese slicer (or
* vegetable peeler)*

Preparing the Fennel: Remove any tough or bruised outer leaves. Cut away feathery tops and root ends. Wash the trimmed bulbs, and slice as thinly as possible. Scatter the fennel over the platter. Season with salt and pepper, and drizzle with 1-½ to 2 tablespoons olive oil.

Preparing the Mushrooms: Shave the mushrooms on the slicer, producing almost transparent cross sections. Strew over the fennel, covering it with an airy layer. Season the mushrooms with more salt and pepper, a good squeeze of lemon juice, and the rest of the olive oil.

Serving: With the cheese slicer (or vegetable peeler), shave about 30 thin slivers of Parmesan on top of the fennel and mushrooms. Serve immediately.

COOK'S NOTES

....

....

....

....

....

....

....

Jacques Pépin

Chef-at-Large

There is no question in Jacques Pépin's mind as to what he likes most about the food profession—the diversity. And few in the field could match him for breadth of experience. Master chef, author of six books and countless articles, professional instructor at Boston University, nationally acclaimed teacher, Dean of Studies at the New York French Culinary Institute, host of his own PBS cooking shows, consultant—he does it all.

Jacques began his remarkable career at thirteen apprenticing at the Hôtel de L'Europe in his hometown of Bourg-en-Bresse. That he had grown up in a restaurant family did not save him from the then tedious life of the apprentice. "You worked next to the chef but he didn't explain anything—just said 'chop the parsley, trim the meat, clean up the floor.' For a year you're not allowed near the stove. Then one day the chef says, 'You start to work at the stove' and you don't think you know anything. But when you get there you find you know it; you learned by osmosis." Jacques knew it well indeed and went on to work in Paris at the Meurice, the Plaza-Athénée, and as personal chef to two prime ministers and to president Charles de Gaulle.

He moved to the United States in 1959 and into the kitchen of New York's Le Pavillon, and from there to Howard Johnson as director of research and development. Somehow he found time to instruct skiing, earn a master's degree from Columbia University in French literature, and take up painting.

Chef Jacques is constantly teaching, demonstrating his technical virtuosity, as he crisscrosses the country approximately thirty times a year. "When you become a good cook, you become a good craftsman first. You repeat and repeat and repeat until your hands know how to move without having to think about it." Jacques demonstrated his culinary dexterity to us with two splendid recipes—modern versions of classic cuisine.

Puff Pastry

Puff pastry "puffs" because of the way it is rolled out and folded, then rolled and folded again, and again, and again, until it consists of hundreds of layers of dough sandwiched between hundreds of layers of butter; when it is baked, each layer of dough puffs up between the layers of butter, which, of course, makes the whole baked structure puff. Puff pastry makes wonderfully buttery flaky tender eating, and is thus the dough for vol-au-vent pastry cases, tart shells, puffy mouthfuls for cocktail appetizers, and lightly crunchy cookie concoctions. It is certainly worthwhile for any serious cook to have it in his or her repertoire, since, once made, it can sit in your freezer for months, hoping you will call upon it for some great occasion. In addition, it's fun to make, and just the making of it teaches anyone the essential feel of pastry doughs.

Warning: Give yourself plenty of time if you are new to pastry. You are working on a dough with high butter content, and that butter must remain cold while you are working on it. Many recipes for puff pastry, by the way, use even more butter—here the proportions are 3 units butter to 4 flour, but 4 butter to 4 flour requires even more attention to the cold factor. Whatever your proportions, if the dough softens and becomes limp while you are working on it, stop where you are and refrigerate everything for 20 minutes or so, then continue. Working rapidly and/or keeping the dough cold are the real secrets to puff pastry. With those two points well in mind, you can take your time and enjoy yourself. You will gain speed with practice, and when you eventually work with the rapidity and confidence of Jacques Pépin, your dough will never have time to soften.

Puff Pastry (continued)

INGREDIENTS FOR
2-¼ POUNDS
(ENOUGH FOR 2 OF CHEF
JACQUES'S PASTRY CASES,
PLUS ABOUT I POUND OF
VALUABLE LEFTOVERS)

*3 cups (about 1 pound)
unbleached all-purpose
flour (plus a little more as
needed)*

1 teaspoon salt

*9 ounces (1 cup plus 2
tablespoons) very cold water
(plus droplets more if
needed)*

*3 sticks (12 ounces) chilled
unsalted butter, each stick
cut into 4 lengthwise slices
of equal size*

SPECIAL EQUIPMENT
SUGGESTED

*A food processor with steel
blade (not essential)*

*A rolling pin with rolling
surface at least 16 inches
long*

Mixing the Dough: Measure the flour, salt, and cup of water into the bowl of the food processor and process just until the mixture masses into a fairly soft dough—if too dry, process in droplets more water; if too damp, process in a tablespoon or so more flour. Avoid overprocessing, since overworking the dough can make it rubbery. (Or make the dough by hand.) Turn the dough out onto a lightly floured work surface, and with your rolling pin rapidly roll it into a 9- by 15-inch rectangle less than ⅛-inch thick.

Folding in the Butter: Leaving a ½-inch border of dough free at the edges of the rectangle, neatly and lightly press 2 rows of 6 chilled butter slices close together over the upper two-thirds of the rectangle. Bring the lower unbuttered third of the rectangle up and over the lower half of the butter slices, and gently flip the butter-laden top third over to cover it.

You now have a 5- by 9-inch rectangle consisting of a bottom layer of dough, a layer of butter slices, a second layer of dough, a second layer of butter slices, and a third or top layer of dough. Pound the rectangle lightly but firmly with your rolling pin to start extending it, and then roll it on your lightly floured surface to form an 11- by 20-inch rectangle about ½-inch thick.

Fold both the short ends of the rectangle in to meet at the center, and then fold the dough in half again at this center line. This "double turn" now gives you 8 layers of butter between 9 layers of dough. Repeat the rolling and folding procedure for a second double turn. Wrap and refrigerate the dough at this point for 20 minutes at least, to relax the dough and to chill it. Give it two more double turns, then wrap and refrigerate it for at least 20 minutes more, and it is ready to use.

Ahead-of-Time Note: Puff pastry will keep 2 to 3 days in the refrigerator, and can be frozen for months. If you know you are preparing a dough for freezing, freeze it before the final two turns and you will get a higher rise.

Vol-au-Vent—Puff Pastry Case

The classic vol-au-vent, delicious and impressive though it may be, is definitely something of a construction job, involving a lot of pastry, a lot of butter, and a lot of work. Chef Jacques's ingenious alternative is far easier to execute, being a thin bottom disk of puff pastry dough on which sets a ball of aluminum foil over which he drapes a thin puff pastry topping. When baked, the ball of foil is removed and—voilà!—you have a vol-au-vent worthy of holding the most marvelous of concoctions, including such delicacies as Pépin-braised sweetbreads in truffle sauce.

Making the Vol-au-Vent: Preheat the oven so that it is at 400° F at baking time.

Line a cookie sheet with parchment paper. Working rapidly from now on, so the dough will not soften too much, roll the chilled puff pastry into a thin rectangle about 24 inches long and 12 inches wide. Cut off a 12-inch piece, roll it up on your pin, and unroll it over the parchment paper. Crush a piece of foil to make a ball about 7 inches across and 2 inches high. Place it in the middle of the dough on the cookie sheet; with the pastry brush paint the surrounding dough lightly with cold water. Cut a 2-inch strip off the remaining dough and set aside for decorations, then drape the rest of the dough over the ball of foil, stretching it down gently to cover the ball and to make a 1-inch border all around its circumference on the bottom piece of dough. Press this border firmly in place with your fingers to glue the two doughs together.

To make a neat circular shape, set the 9-inch ring (or bowl or pan) in place over the structure, and cut off excess dough from around it. To seal the circumference of the case, press the flat side of the tines of a table fork an inch around the edge, leaving a decorative border.

INGREDIENTS FOR 6 TO 8 SERVINGS

1-¼ pounds chilled puff pastry (preceding recipe)

Egg wash (1 egg, minus ½ the white, beaten in a small bowl with ½ teaspoon water)

SPECIAL EQUIPMENT SUGGESTED

A cookie sheet

Parchment paper

A rolling pin with rolling surface at least 16 inches long

Aluminum foil

A pastry brush

A pastry ring (or deep bowl or pan), 9 inches across

A cookie cutter (or the end of a pastry tube), about 1 inch across

A serrated knife

Vol-au-Vent (continued)

Decorations: Cut decorations out of the reserved dough: a strip ⅜-inches wide from the length, 1-inch rectangles, disks made with the large end of the pastry tube or a cookie cutter. With the pastry brush paint the vol-au-vent with a coating of egg wash. Encircle the middle of the vol-au-vent with the long strip of dough to mark the eventual cover and press the decorations around the lower part. Pierce a ¼-inch steam hole in the very top, and surround with a pretty twist of dough. Just before baking, paint with a final coat of egg wash, and make shallow knife cuts in downward swirls from top to middle—like the cuts for a *pithiviers,* the classic French almond tart.

Baking the Vol-au-Vent—30 minutes: Set in the lower middle level of the preheated 400° F oven, and bake for 30 minutes, or until the pastry has browned nicely and is crisp around the edges; lift gently to see if the bottom has also crisped and browned. Remove from the oven and let cool for 10 minutes or so.

Removing the Cover: Very carefully, with a sawing motion of your serrated knife, cut around the underside of the encircling pastry strip, and lift off the cover. Again with great care, remove the ball of foil.

Serving Vol-au-Vent: Fill the vol-au-vent only at the last moment, so that the pastry will remain crisp, and set the cover askew over the filling.

Ahead-of-Time Note: Puff pastry is always at its best when freshly baked. If it is to wait, keep it in a warming oven if you have one. Otherwise, set it aside and reheat it by heating the oven to 400° F, turning it off, and placing the puff pastry inside. Or freeze it—baked puff pastry freezes well.

Leftover Puff Pastry: Jacques Pépin gathers his strips together and saves them in the freezer until he has enough to make a flaky pie crust.

COOK'S NOTES

Braised Sweetbreads in Puff Pastry with Truffle Sauce

This is a splendid example of modern classic French cuisine, something you can rarely enjoy in these times of minimalist cookery and minimum time. It's an elaborate recipe, definitely one for those who love to serve marvelous dishes to their friends and enjoy the mechanics of real cooking. A great deal of the parts, however, may be done well in advance, so that the finale comes off with relative ease. For example, the rich brown stock for the truffled sauce can be cooked and waiting for you in the freezer, as well as the puff pastry for the vol-au-vent pastry case and the vol-au-vent itself, while the braising of the sweetbreads may be done the day before.

Preparing the Sweetbreads:

Soaking and Blanching. If the sweetbreads have not been presoaked (you can tell, since rather than being creamy white and unblemished they will have bloody spots), they will then need soaking as follows: Set in a large bowl of cold water for 12 hours (or overnight), changing the water several times, until they have whitened. Remove from the water and place in a saucepan, adding 2 quarts water. Bring to the boil over high heat, and boil 1 minute. Drain, and set again in the large bowl, filled with fresh cold water to cover, until they have cooled completely.

Trimming and Pressing. Pull off and discard most of the outside sinews, but do not go too deeply and damage the essential shape. Arrange the sweetbreads on a tray (or cookie sheet) lined with a double thickness of paper towels, and cover with another layer of paper towels, a second tray or baking sheet, and a 5-pound weight of some sort (like several cans of corned beef hash). Refrigerate for several hours (or overnight).

Braising—About 40 minutes. Season the sweetbreads with a light sprinkling of salt and pepper. Set the pan (or casserole) over moderately high heat, swirl in 2 tablespoons butter, and when the butter foam has begun to subside lay in the sweetbreads. Let them cook for 2 to 3 minutes on each side, or until they are nicely browned and beginning to stick a bit to the bottom of the pan where juices are starting to coagulate. Pour in the

INGREDIENTS FOR 6 SERVINGS AS A MAIN COURSE

For braising the sweetbreads

3 pounds veal sweetbreads cut into serving pieces (see box)

½ teaspoon salt

¼ teaspoon freshly ground black pepper

2 tablespoons unsalted butter

½ cup strong brown chicken stock (see page 133)

⅓ cup dry white wine

(continued)

Sweetbreads (continued)

For the sauce
Aromatic flavoring:
2 medium-sized celery stalks
 (tender white ribs)
2 medium-sized leeks (white
 and tender green parts)
1 large peeled carrot
2 tablespoons butter
⅓ cup water
Final reduction and liaison:
3 cups strong brown chicken
 stock, see page 133
⅔ cup dry Madeira, Sercial or
 Verdehlo (or dry sherry)
1 teaspoon potato starch
 blended with 1 tablespoon
 Madeira (or dry sherry)
1 tablespoon dark soy sauce

For the truffle (optional but
 highly desirable)
1 large fresh black truffle
 (Tuberum malenosporum),
 or a canned truffle and its
 juices
1 tablespoon cognac

For the vol-au-vent
 (see preceding recipe)

stock and white wine, cover the pan, and let simmer gently for about 30 minutes, until the sweetbreads are tender when pierced with a sharp-pronged fork and the surrounding juices are reduced to a glaze. Set aside.

Finishing the Sauce: While the sweetbreads are braising, cut the celery, leeks, and carrot into *brunoise*—very fine, neat ⅛-inch dice—and turn them into a saucepan with 2 tablespoons butter and ⅓ cup water. Cover and simmer 10 minutes, or until tender. Meanwhile, in a 2-quart saucepan start slowly boiling down the stock and the Madeira (or sherry); when it has reduced to about 2 cups, taste carefully for seasoning. Remove from heat and stir in the starch mixture; return the saucepan to the heat, stirring rather slowly while the sauce thickens slightly. Stir in the soy sauce for color, then the cooked *brunoise* of vegetables. Simmer briefly, check seasoning again, and set aside.

Start preheating the oven to 400° F.

Preparing the Truffle (For more information about truffles, see Appendix, page 137): 30 minutes before serving, peel the rough outer skin from the truffle, chop the peelings, and mix in a small bowl with the truffle juices (if using a canned truffle) and the cognac. Using a vegetable peeler, cut the truffle into slivers, and set aside. About 10 minutes before serving, bring the sauce to a boil, add the chopped truffle peelings and their soaking juices, cover, and simmer for 1 minute.

SWEETBREAD NOTES

There are two types of sweetbreads—the long, narrow thymus sweetbread, and the smoother, rounder pancreas sweetbread. Jacques Pépin prefers the latter if he is offered the choice. Many markets do not carry sweetbreads at all, and often if you order them you have to take a 5-pound frozen package. Shop around in ethnic markets, where they are more likely to be. By the way, we raise beautiful veal with beautiful sweetbreads in this country, but there is so little call here for such delicacies as sweetbreads and brains that they are usually sent abroad.

Serving: Meanwhile, cover the sweetbread pan and set in the preheated oven to warm through. When the sweetbreads are ready, place the vol-au-vent shell on the platter and set the pastry cover aside. Spoon sweetbreads into the vol-au-vent and arrange some decoratively around the outside. Rapidly pour the sauce into the sweetbread pan to deglaze it, then spoon some sauce over the sweetbreads and pour the rest into a warm sauceboat to be passed separately. Spread the truffle slices over the sweetbread pieces, set the vol-au-vent cover askew over the pastry for presentation flair, and serve at once.

SPECIAL EQUIPMENT SUGGESTED

A heavy-bottomed pan or casserole, about 12 inches across and 3 inches deep, for the braising

A vegetable peeler

A warmed serving platter, such as a 10- by 14-inch oval

A sauceboat, warmed

Lobster Soufflé à l'Américaine

Here is another recipe from the glorious past, first made famous by the Hôtel Plaza-Athénée in Paris but based on a great Parisian lobster dish of the 1800s, *Homard à l'Américaine*—lobster sautéed with tomatoes and cognac. In the Plaza-Athénée version, the sautéed and sauced lobster is arranged in the bottom of a soufflé dish, and the soufflé is baked on top of it. Chef Jacques feels the lobster becomes overcooked this way; he therefore steams the lobster briefly, makes his sauce out of the shells, and cooks a cheese soufflé separately to accompany them. This recipe, therefore, treats each part separately and then joins them together for the final presentation.

INGREDIENTS FOR 4 SERVINGS

For the lobster

4 live lobsters, about 1-½ pounds each

2 tablespoons softened unsalted butter

For the lobster stock

3 tablespoons olive oil

1 large onion, peeled and roughly cut

1 large celery stalk, roughly cut

1 medium carrot, unpeeled, scrubbed, and roughly cut

6 large cloves garlic, unpeeled and crushed

(continued)

Steaming the Lobsters—12 minutes: Place 4 cups water in the wok (or kettle) and bring to the boil over high heat. Meanwhile, remove the rubber bands surrounding the lobster claws and set two lobsters in each tier of the bamboo steamer (or all four in the kettle). Bring the water to a rolling boil, cover closely, and steam for 12 minutes. The lobsters are not completely cooked but done enough so that the meat can be removed from the shells. Transfer the lobsters to a tray or roasting pan and let cool briefly. Reserve 2 cups of the cooking liquid in the wok.

Removing the Lobster Meat: One by one, hold the lobsters over a bowl to catch their juices while you twist off the big claws, joints, and tails. Crack the lob-

sters open and remove tail, claw, and joint meat. Cut a shallow slit along the outside curve of the tail meat; remove and discard the intestinal vein. Remove the uncooked loose tomalley (green matter) from the chests, add the soft butter; press through the sieve into the small saucepan, scraping off the bottom of the sieve to include every last bit of tomalley; reserve.

For decoration, retain 2 chest shells with eyes and head and the final flap sections of the tails. Chop up the other chest shells and small legs, and reserve for the sauce base. Discard remaining shells.

You should have about 2-½ cups of meat; arrange it in the gratin dish, cover with a clean, damp towel, and refrigerate. You should also have the juices from opening the lobsters and the lobster-steaming liquid. Strain each through a fine-meshed sieve and taste. If one is too salty, dilute it with the other (or discard and substitute plain chicken stock). You should have about 3-½ cups of liquid in all.

Preparing the Lobster Stock—40 minutes: Set the large saucepan over moderately high heat, add the oil, and when hot stir in the chopped vegetables. Sauté to soften and brown lightly, stirring with a wooden spoon, for 4 to 5 minutes. Add the chopped chests and legs, and sauté 3 to 4 minutes. Pour in 2 tablespoons of the cognac and ignite, shaking the pan. Douse the flames with the wine, and the reserved lobster liquid. Stir in the diced tomato, tomato sauce, and seasonings. Bring to the simmer, cover, and simmer for 30 minutes. Pour into the colander, shaking to dislodge juices from the shells, then strain into the saucepan and boil down, until reduced to 1-½ cups.

Finishing the Sauce: Add the cream to the reduced liquid, and stir in the dissolved potato starch. Continue to cook, stirring constantly for 1 minute or so, until the sauce has thickened. Stir in the remaining tablespoon of cognac, and set aside. Reheat just before serving.

Preparing the Tomalley: Set the tomalley in its saucepan over low heat, stirring until it warms through but does not come near the boil. If there is sufficient roe, the tomalley will turn a luscious salmon pink; stir it into the sauce before serving. If not, reserve to pass with the lobster. In any case, taste for seasoning and stir in a teaspoon of cognac.

Preparing the Soufflé (see following recipe, Freestanding Cheese Soufflé).

3 tablespoons cognac (2 for the sauce base, 1 to finish the sauce)

1 cup dry white wine

1 large tomato cut into 1-inch dice

1 cup tomato sauce, fresh or canned

2 teaspoons herbes de Provence (or Italian herb seasoning)

3 imported bay leaves

2 teaspoons paprika

2 tablespoons chopped fresh tarragon (leaves and stems)

½ teaspoon cayenne pepper

½ teaspoon fennel seeds

To finish the lobster sauce

½ cup heavy cream

1-½ teaspoons potato starch dissolved in 2 tablespoons water

1 teaspoon cognac (for the tomalley)

For serving

The cheese soufflé (recipe follows)

A handful of fresh chives, some chopped and some whole

(continued)

Lobster Soufflé (continued)

**SPECIAL EQUIPMENT
SUGGESTED**

*A wok and two-tiered bamboo
  steamer (or a steamer
  basket and large covered
  kettle)*

A colander set over a bowl

*A fine-meshed sieve set over a
  small saucepan*

*A gratin dish, about 9 by 12
  inches*

*A 4-quart, heavy-bottomed
  saucepan*

*A large round serving platter
  (or 4 soup plates), warmed*

A sauceboat, warmed

Reheating the Lobster Meat: Remove the lobster meat from the refrigerator. About 12 minutes before the soufflé is finished, place the lobster meat in the oven alongside the soufflé to warm the meat through.

Serving: Move rapidly from this point on. Run a knife around the soufflé and open the spring on the pan. Remove the sides of the pan, but leave the bottom in place. Place the soufflé (still on the pan bottom) in the center of the warmed platter. Arrange the lobster around the soufflé and spoon half the sauce over the lobster, pouring the rest into the warmed sauceboat to pass separately. Decorate the platter with the reserved lobster bodies and tail pieces. Sprinkle the chopped chives on top, and decorate with whole chives. Serve immediately.

Alternative Serving Method: Place equal amounts of the lobster meat in the bottom of four soup plates, and spoon on the hot sauce. Sprinkle with the chives, and heap a generous portion of the soufflé into the center of each bowl. Serve at once.

COOK'S NOTES

Freestanding Cheese Soufflé

Baked in a ring mold, this fine otherwise traditional cheese soufflé can stand alone on a platter, or can be surrounded as in this case by the magnificent preceding Lobster *à l'Américaine.*

Coating the Spring-form Pan: Smear the softened butter all over the pan, particularly over the sides. In a small bowl, blend the fresh bread crumbs, Parmesan cheese, and paprika. Pour into the buttered pan and roll the pan around in your hands to coat the bottom and especially the sides.

Preparing the Béchamel Base for the Soufflé: Preheat the oven to 375° F. Melt the chilled butter in a 3-quart saucepan and blend in the flour. Cook the roux for several seconds, until it froths and bubbles. Remove from heat for a few seconds, until the bubbling stops, then pour in all the milk at once, whisking vigorously to blend it and the roux. Return to

INGREDIENTS FOR 4 SERVINGS

For coating the soufflé dish
1 to 2 teaspoons softened unsalted butter
3 tablespoons fresh bread crumbs
1 tablespoon grated Parmesan cheese
1 teaspoon paprika

(continued)

Cheese Soufflé (continued)

For the soufflé

*3 tablespoons chilled unsalted
   butter*

3 tablespoons all-purpose flour

1 cup warm milk

3 egg yolks

5 egg whites

*1 cup grated Swiss cheese
   (preferably Gruyère)*

*2 tablespoons grated Parmesan
   cheese*

**SPECIAL EQUIPMENT
SUGGESTED**

*A spring-form pan, 8 inches
   across and 2-½ to 3 inches
   deep*

heat and bring to the boil, whisking while the sauce thickens—it will be very thick. Remove from the heat and whisk in the 3 egg yolks.

Preparing the Egg Whites: Beat the egg whites to stiff shining peaks (see page 134). Stir ⅓ into the hot soufflé base to lighten it, then scrape the base into one side of the egg whites. Rapidly and delicately, fold them together, sprinkling in the Swiss cheese as you do so.

Baking the Soufflé—35 minutes: At once, scoop the soufflé into the prepared pan. Sprinkle the Parmesan cheese on top, and set in the lower third level of the preheated oven. Bake for 30 to 35 minutes, until the soufflé has risen and browned nicely. It must be firm enough to stand alone when unmolded; a straw, plunged down through the center, should come out almost clean.

Serving: Unmold as directed in the preceding lobster recipe.

COOK'S NOTES

STRONG BROWN CHICKEN STOCK—*DEMI-GLACE*

This is the modern classic French way to a fine strong brown stock, the kind you want for accompaniment to a splendid dish of braised sweetbreads, such as those on page 125. In traditional French cooking, a *demi-glace* is always the final long-simmered stage of the classic, even longer simmered roux-thickened espagnole, which in turn is based on the classic long-simmered brown stock. Many contemporary chefs have dispensed with the roux and the old *demi-glace* in favor of a fine, strong, well-reduced stock and a light starch thickener if needed. This particular stock of Chef Jacques's is an excellent example.

INGREDIENTS FOR ABOUT I QUART

4 pounds chicken neck and carcass bones, including raw veal bones if available
  (order in advance, or collect in your freezer)
2-½ cups unpeeled, roughly diced onions
1-½ cups unpeeled, scrubbed, roughly diced carrots
1 cup roughly diced celery
½ cup plain tomato sauce, fresh or canned
3 imported bay leaves
2 teaspoons herbes de Provence (or Italian herb seasoning)
1 teaspoon black peppercorns

SPECIAL EQUIPMENT SUGGESTED

A large roasting pan
An 8-quart stockpot
A skimmer and a large spoon
A colander set over a large bowl
A fine-meshed sieve
A 1-½-quart covered container

Spread the bones in a single layer in the roasting pan and brown in a 400° F oven for 40 minutes or more, until they are a dark mahogany brown, stirring occasionally. Add onions and carrots and continue browning another 30 minutes. Transfer the solids from the roasting pan to the stockpot, and discard any fat from the pan.

Deglaze the roasting pan by pouring in 1 quart water, setting it over heat, and stirring with a wooden spoon, reaching all over the bottom of the pan until all the solidified roasting juices have dissolved. Pour deglazing liquid into the stockpot along with 5 quarts water and bring to the simmer. Skim off and discard scum and fat, which will continue rising to the surface for 15 minutes or so.

Add the celery, tomato sauce, bay leaves, herbs, and black peppercorns to the stockpot, bring back to the simmer, and simmer gently, uncovered, for 3-½ hours.

Pour the stock through the colander into the bowl, pressing juices out of ingredients. Then pour the resulting liquid from the bowl through the sieve into a 1-½-quart container. When cool, cover and refrigerate.

Before proceeding, remove solidified fat from the top of the cold stock, which will jell when chilled.

Ahead-of-Time Note: Stock will keep 2 to 3 days in the refrigerator; defatted stock may be frozen for weeks.

Appendix

Techniques

BEATING EGG WHITES

A good number of egg whites are beaten in this book, some by machine and some by hand. The aim is for perfectly beaten whites that rise some 7 times their original volume and hold themselves in stiff shining peaks. Here's what to watch for:

A Clean Separation: Be sure there is no speck of yolk in the egg whites, since that can hinder the rise.

A Clean Bowl and Beater: Be absolutely sure there is no oil or grease on either the bowl or beater. Wash and dry both, then put a teaspoon of salt and a tablespoon of vinegar in the bowl and rub all over with paper towels, rubbing the beater also. Wipe both clean but do not wash them, since the faint vinegar residue will help to stabilize the egg whites.

Room Temperature: Set the bowl for 1 minute or so in a larger bowl of hot water to take off the chill and your egg whites will mount higher and faster.

Relation of Bowl to Beater: You want the whole mass of egg whites to be involved—in other words, use a large beater in a small bowl. The balloon whip and copper bowl used by Jacques Pépin on page 120 are ideal. A heavy-duty tabletop electric mixer with large whip that rotates around itself as it rotates around the bowl is also ideal. Otherwise, you can use a portable electric mixer with double whisks, and rotate it around the bowl as though you yourself were the aforementioned tabletop model.

The Method: Chef Jacques directs, whether you are beating by hand or machine, that you start fast for a few seconds, to break up the globular mass of the egg whites, then slow down, until the whites have begun to foam. Gradually increase speed, until the whites form stiff shining peaks.

Be very careful and watchful with a fast machine that you don't overbeat, or the egg whites will break down, begin to look grainy, and lose both their staying power and their puffing ability. (If this does happen, however, beat in another white, which will bring them back to usable form.)

BEATING WHOLE EGGS AND SUGAR

Many recipes instruct you to beat an egg mixture until "it forms the ribbon." This means that the eggs must triple in volume, look like a thick, soft, pale yellow mayonnaise, and when a big dollop is lifted up it falls back on the surface in a slowly dissolving ribbon. Eggs and sugar beaten this way are used in such basics as Génoise sponge cakes and dessert sauces, and are fundamentals in any serious cook's pastry and dessert repertoire.

Hand Beating: Jan Birnbaum beats egg yolks and citrus syrup over hot water for zabaglione sauce. He, like Michel Richard for chocolate melting, uses the chef-type double boiler: an 8-inch saucepan with 2 inches of simmering water over which he sets a tight-fitting stainless steel bowl. In go the eggs and sugar (honey in this case), and he beats them with a large wire whisk at a leisurely pace for about 5 minutes, until they are warm to the finger and have formed a thick, soft, tripled-in-volume mass.

Machine Beating: The same bowl-to-beater relationship applies here as it does to beating egg whites. Be sure to warm the eggs to room temperature before you begin, then add the sugar and beat at moderately fast speed for 5 minutes or so.

PAN-SEARING MEAT

Meat that is seared in a heavy pan on top of the stove develops a delicious, caramelized crust and retains a nice juicy center. It's a good, quick way to prepare small cuts of meat and has the great advantage of depositing tasty juices in the pan for a sauce.

Pat the meat thoroughly dry with paper towels. Get the pan very hot and then film the bottom with oil. Lay the pieces of meat in the pan away from you, so that the fat will not splatter on you. Do not crowd the pan or the meat will steam and not form a crust; use two pans if necessary, or cook the meat in two batches. There should be at least ½ inch of space between the pieces of meat. When one side of the meat is browned, turn and sear the other side. Test the meat by poking it with your finger: rare meat should feel springy, with a slight resistance, not squashy like raw meat.

BRUNOISE VS. MIREPOIX

Serious cooks should learn culinary terms, especially those that are used regularly in professional kitchens. It's an efficient short-cut language that speeds up communication.

"Brunoise" and *"mirepoix"* are two terms that are often confused. *Brunoise* refers to a size and shape of cut; it is a fine, tiny dice. Anything—vegetables, meat, poultry—can be cut into *brunoise,* although the term is used most often in reference to vegetables. Ingredients cut *à la brunoise* are usually sautéed in butter or oil to be used as the base for soups or sauces.

Mirepoix indicates a combination of carrots, celery, and onions and may be cut into any size. Quarter-inch dice are usually sautéed as a flavoring and garnish for soups and sauces, or for braised foods. Large dice (or coarsely chopped) vegetables are those to be strewn around a piece of meat or fish to add flavor to the braising liquid or soup base. In the old days a *mirepoix* also contained ham or bacon; today it is optional and chefs indicate its addition by asking for a *mirepoix gras* or "fat vegetable mix." These are called for to flavor hearty dishes whereas a lean mixture, *mirepoix maigre,* is for more delicate foods.

MAKING CANDIED CITRUS ZEST

The zest of citrus fruit is the colored part of the peel only—the white pith is bitter and unsightly. Either use a zester (a knife-shaped instrument whose blunt metal end is punctured with sharp little holes; when drawn down the peel it comes off in thin julienne curls), or remove the peel in 2-inch strips and cut into very thin julienne with a very sharp knife.

To candy, blanch the zest of two oranges three times by dropping them into a pan with 2 cups of boiling water for several seconds, draining and rinsing them, and repeating the process with fresh water. The third time, drop them into a light sugar syrup (1 cup of sugar brought to the simmer and dissolved in 1 cup of water). Simmer 10 minutes or more, until the syrup has thickened and drops from the spoon in a thick thread.

Ahead-of-Time Note: Zests will keep perfectly in their syrup for weeks; store in a covered jar in the refrigerator. To use, spread on wax paper to dry.

TOASTING CUMIN, CORIANDER, AND OTHER SPICES

Toasted spice seeds are called for by many chefs, since toasting will intensify the flavor. Toss the seeds in a dry frying pan for several seconds over moderate heat, until they brown or change color. Use as is or grind in a spice mill or electric blender.

MUSHROOMS: TRIMMING, WASHING, AND MACHINE CHOPPING

Shave off and discard the ends of the mushroom stems. If the mushrooms are clean and the caps are closed around the tops of the stems, simply brush them to remove any sand. If they seem dirty or if the caps are open, do not hesitate to wash them: drop them into a large bowl of cold water, and at once swish them about with your hands, let sit 10 seconds, then remove with your hands (allowing any sand to remain at the bottom of the bowl) and pat dry in a towel. If you machine-chop, first roughly chop the mushrooms by hand.

Machine Chopping (for duxelles and other preparations): The food processor is fine for this, but if the mushrooms are whole or if you add too many at a time you will get part mush and part chop. If your recipe also includes shallots or herbs, roughly chop them first. Turn on the machine and drop them in, then proceed with a big handful of your roughly chopped mushrooms, using the on-off pulse technique and watching closely—it goes fast and 5 or 6 pulses are usually enough. Remove from the machine and proceed with the rest.

DEGREASING A STOCK OR A SAUCE

You can, of course, skim the fat off the surface with a spoon, an often long and never completely efficient process. Another and better solution is to buy a degreasing pitcher with its spout opening at the bottom. Pour in the hot liquid, wait a moment until the fat has risen to the surface, then pour off the fat-free liquid and stop just before the fat appears in the spout. Or, when you have time, refrigerate the stock or sauce and peel off the layer of fat when it has congealed on top.

Ingredients

CRÈME FRAÎCHE

Crème fraîche is the traditional unpasteurized French heavy cream that, when allowed to mature, thickens into a mayonnaiselike cream and takes on a pleasant lightly sour taste. It is used to thicken and enrich sauces, such as those for fillets of sole poached in white wine, veal scallops with mushrooms, and so forth. *Crème fraîche* by itself also accompanies fresh-fruit desserts, baked apples, and the like. It was tremendously popular here in the states, especially during the 1960s and 70s, but its popularity waned with growing nutritional fears in the 80s.

BLACK TRUFFLES

At almost $400 a pound the rare fresh black truffle, *tuberum malenosporum,* might well be considered a status symbol as well as a treasure. Fortunately, when you choose carefully, just one of these "black diamonds" of less than an ounce is sufficient to perfume a whole dish.

A superb, fully mature fresh black truffle is firm with no blemishes and has a pleasant aroma of truffle—which is like nothing else. When it is cut open the inside is dark gray with a filigree of white. Overripe truffles have an unpleasantly strong, earthy decaying smell. Underripe ones have little or no truffle smell, and a whitish color at the center.

Fresh truffles are perishable, and the aroma is fleeting. Before using a fresh truffle, scrub it with a vegetable brush under warm water. It will be covered with a thick, rough, wrinkled skin that should be removed with a vegetable peeler or small very sharp knife. Dice the skin pieces very fine and use them to flavor eggs, pâtés, sauces, and the like. Use the peeled truffle as directed in whatever recipe you are preparing.

To store whole fresh truffles, wrap in several layers of plastic plus a firmly closing plastic bag or a screw-topped jar. Refrigerate up to six days or store in the freezer for several months. Leftover pieces of truffle may be submerged in broth, Madeira, or cognac and refrigerated for a month.

Canned truffles will also last in the refrigerator for a month or more.

Canned truffles have been cooked either once or twice to stabilize them. Buy the ones that have been cooked only once—*1ère cuisson* on the can. Canned peelings are also available for adding truffle flavor to sauces and eggs.

An informative illustrated rundown on truffles is in Jacques Pépin's book, *The Art of Cooking, Volume 2* (Knopf).

OLIVE OIL

Selecting olive oil is an ongoing process, since it comes from many places, including France, Italy, Spain, Greece, and California. There is a great to-do about "virgin" and "extra virgin" olive oil. Virgin is presumed to mean it is oil extracted from the first cold pressing of the olives, while extra virgin presumably means the oil was extracted from selected—even hand-picked—ripe olives. There are no laws enforcing any of this, and you can spend an extravagant amount. What you are looking for is a good fruity, fresh taste and aroma that appeals to you. The only way to tell is to sample them yourself, or to get advice from an experienced and knowing friend.

Buy from a market that has a fast turnover and stores its olive oil away from heat and sunlight. At home, keep the bulk of your oil in a tightly closed container in a dark cool place. Pour small amounts that will be used up quickly into an attractive container if you wish.

Use expensive olive oils sparingly and for flavor—in salads and for finishing dishes where just a small amount is sufficient. Use lesser-grade oils—still with a pure, clean flavor—for cooking.

Try making Alice Waters's garlic croutons as a good way to use your best olive oil. Once her country bread is toasted, she rubs one side with a cut clove of garlic and drizzles on her best olive oil—a real treat.

SALSIFY, OYSTER PLANT, SCORZONERA

The potato salsify pie on page 98 that goes with Jan Birnbaum's roasted leg of lamb brings up the whole question of salsify and what is it, anyway? Salsify and its cousin, scorzonera, are carrot-shaped root vegetables with a pleasantly mild, almost sweet flavor; like carrots, they taste like nothing else but themselves. To some, however, the flavor suggests that of oysters, which is why they are also called oyster plant. Salsify is white-skinned, scorzonera is a blackish brown; they are similar in flavor, and many make no distinction—thus, both are called salsify. You will rarely if ever see either vegetable in our general supermarket, but I was happy to find salsify the other day in one of our specialty fruit-and-vegetable stores.

My best source for such questions is the late Jane Grigson's *Vegetable Book* (New York: Atheneum, 1979)—alas, out of print—since it is a wonderfully valuable and authentic compendium. She gives recipes for salsify soups, salads, pies and fritters, as well as for plain whole cooked salsify (or scorzonera), which is what you want in Birnbaum's recipe. Grigson cautions you to choose only fairly smooth roots that are firm to the touch. Top and tail them, and scrub the roots clean with a brush under a running tap. You can then peel (or scrape) the roots and drop them into acidulated water so they will not discolor, then cook them with the potatoes as in the Birnbaum recipe. Or, after scrubbing, simmer them whole in lightly salted water for about ½ hour, or until just tender, then refresh in cold water, peel them, and they are ready to use.

Tools/Kitchen Know-How

Cheesecloth: Cheesecloth is a frequent aid in cooking—for wrapping a chicken or tying up an herb bouquet, for instance. Because it often contains a sizing and/or has a medicinal taste, always wash in warm water and soap and rinse well before using.

Herb Bouquet (Bouquet Garni): This is a packet of herbs tied together so that the packet can be removed easily and the herbs will not float around and disperse themselves in the food. If you have enough leaves in the bouquet, use them as a covering; otherwise, tie them all together in washed cheesecloth. The usual bouquet consists of thyme, parsley stems, and bay leaves, but your recipe may specify the addition of celery leaves, garlic, or whatever.

Note on Bay Leaves: California bay leaves have a strong, rather oily taste, quite different from Turkish or Mediterranean bay *Laurus nobilis.* If your recipe does not specify, you are always safe using the Turkish bay.

White Butcher's Twine (Corned Beef Twine): A pliable white cotton twine with no sizing, odor, or flavor used by butchers to truss meats and chickens. Ask your butcher for some (or ask where to buy it), or try your local hardware or cookware store.

Special Slicers, Graters, Julienne Tools, et cetera: You can now find a number of small tools that will ease such kitchen jobs as fine-slicing cucumbers and potatoes, julienning carrots, grating ginger, and the like. The heavy and capable French steel mandoline will do a number of these tasks but costs well over

$200. You will find inexpensive, lightweight plastic or wooden slicers and graters in most cookware and hardware stores; all our chefs are using them. To slice the vegetables paper-thin for her fennel salad, Alice Waters, for example, used a small wooden vegetable slicer that she found in a Japanese market.

To Season a Wok, or Any New Stainless Steel or Rusty Iron Pan: Clean and scrub the wok or pan thoroughly in hot water with steel wool and scouring powder; rinse well and dry. Rub liberally inside and out with vegetable oil and set for ½ hour in a 300° F oven or over very low heat. Rub clean with paper towels—if more than a trace of rust remains on the towels, then rub with salt until clean. Finish with a very light protective coating of oil, then rub again.

Index

Credits

We would like to acknowledge the following for contributing or loaning props and food, and for lending their kitchens for the photographs:

Bourgeat

Le Creuset

Eliot and Melanie Cutler

Ann and Frank Farella

The Gardener, Berkeley

Bill and Ann Grace

Steven and Jessica Greenes

Hudson Valley Foie Gras

George and Jenifer Lang

Peter and Emily Luchetti

Luna García

Macy's

Joan Nathan

Alan and Stacie Pando

Stags' Leap

Star Fish Market

Vanderbilt & Co.

A Note on the Type

The text of this book was set on the Macintosh in Adobe Garamond. Designed for the Adobe Corporation by Robert Slimbach, the fonts are based on modern renderings of the type first cut by Claude Garamond (c. 1480–1561). Garamond was a pupil of Geoffroy Tory and is believed to have followed the Venetian models, although he introduced a number of important differences, and it is to him we owe the letter which we know as "old style." He gave to his letters a certain elegance and a feeling of movement that won their creator an immediate reputation and the patronage of Francis I of France.

Color separations by Applied Graphics Technologies, Carlstadt, New Jersey
Printed and bound by R.R. Donnelley & Sons, Willard, Ohio
Designed and illustrated by WORKSIGHT